FUN WITH WOODY

GRAHAM FLASHNER

FUN WITH
WOODY

THE
COMPLETE
WOODY **A**LLEN
QUIZ
BOOK

 AN OWL BOOK

HENRY HOLT AND COMPANY   **NEW YORK**

Published by Henry Holt and Company, Inc.,
521 Fifth Avenue, New York, New York 10175.
Published in Canada by Fitzhenry & Whiteside Limited,
195 Allstate Parkway, Markham, Ontario L3R 4T8.

Library of Congress Cataloging-in-Publication Data
Flashner, Graham.
Fun with Woody.
"An Owl book."
Filmography: p.
1. Allen, Woody—Miscellanea.   I. Title.
PN2287.A53F55   1987   791.43'028'0924 [B] 87–8461
ISBN 0-8050-0519-6 (pbk.)

First Edition

Design by Kate Nichols
Printed in the United States of America
10 9 8 7 6 5 4 3 2 1

On Being Funny: Woody Allen and Comedy by Eric
Lax, copyright © 1975 by Eric Lax, reprinted by per-
mission of JCA Literary Agency.

When the Shooting Stops, the Cutting Begins by Ralph
Rosenblum and Robert Karen, copyright © 1979 by
Ralph Rosenblum and Robert Karen, reprinted by per-
mission of the authors.

ISBN 0-8050-0519-6

"If only I had the nerve to do my own jokes. I don't know how much longer I can keep this smile frozen on my face. I'm in the wrong business, I know it."
　　　　　　　—Alvy Singer, Annie Hall

CONTENTS

ACKNOWLEDGMENTS

This book might still be nothing more than a high-concept idea were it not for an enormous amount of aid and cooperation from a large number of people, and it's those people whom I would like to use this space to thank.

For his initial enthusiasm for the idea, and his expert guidance and support throughout the project, I would like to thank my editor at Henry Holt and Company, Peter Bejger.

For their wonderful assistance in providing me with whatever I needed, I would like to thank Jane Martin and Linda Kurland at Rollins-Joffe Productions, Peter Haas and Amy Johnson at PMK, and Nina Barron at Orion Pictures. This assistance, and the photos that accompanied it, would not have been possible without the approval of the star of this book. To Woody Allen, I owe my sincerest appreciation and gratitude.

For their assistance in providing photos, I would like to thank Ernest and Roberta Boehm at Photoreporters, Anton in Diana Nassau's office at United Artists, Ivy Orta at Columbia Pictures, Patricia Bennett at ABC Video Enterprises, and Judy Singer at Warner Brothers.

For additional photos, I would like to thank Howard Mandelbaum at Phototeque, Frederick and Ken at Bettman Archives, Fred Cantey at Wide World Photos, Todd Flashner, Yvonne Halsman, Jerry Ohrlinger's Movie Material Store, The Phil Gersh Agency, Johnny Planko, Clifford Stevens, Ed Robbins at William Morris, Joe Funicello at ICM, Paul Kohner, Myra Post, Robert Littman, David Gershenson, and Jay Julien. And finally, thanks to Hu Blien Advertising and the Foster Grant Corp., and to Elinor Swan at Warner Brothers Records.

A special note of thanks to Milton Goldman at ICM for allowing me to interview Jeff Daniels.

A number of Woody Allen fans were consulted for this book, contributing questions, criticisms, anecdotes, articles, and general suggestions. For his voluminous biographical file on Woody, which will someday be worth millions, I must thank Steven Warshaw, whose loyalty to Mr. Allen is unmatched.

Additional thanks go to Leona and Jesse Flashner, Francine Forbes, Phil Gurin, Matt Mitler, Jeff Sanders, and Rega and Gary Zuckerman.

A general note of thanks to my agent at The Dorese Agency, Alyss Dorese.

An inestimable amount of thanks to Howard Sherman at Howard Sherman Public Relations, who never dreamed his word processor would spawn this book.

Finally, a very warm thank you to my beloved Christine, whose excitement and devotion to the book was as legendary as the patience she exhibited during my long, lonely hours at the word processor. Hopefully, she will never be stumped on a Woody Allen question again.

INTRODUCTION

*H*ow did you respond the last time someone said to you, "Sex without love is an empty experience"?

Had you been a lifelong Woody Allen fan, you may have instinctively countered with, "Yes . . . but as far as empty experiences go, it's one of the best."

Whether you had the sex or not was irrelevant (not to you, perhaps), but chances are if you *did* manage to remember the line, you forgot the movie it came from. (And I can't tell you here; you'll have to read that chapter.)

What I *can* tell you is that, whether you are a Woody Allen aficionado or a novice who has only enjoyed the "early, funny movies," the book you are holding in your hand is your gateway to the funniest lines and scenes from Woody's films, plays, books, and nightclub routines, as well as behind-the-scenes production notes on Woody and his movies.

This book will do more than broaden your appreciation of America's foremost comic artist. Your social life may never be the same.

Because you'll be able to entertain (and trade notes with) your friends, lover(s), relatives, mere acquaintances, and even your boss—with quips and quotes from *all* of Woody Allen's creative works. You'll be able to stop strangers on the street, at trendy boutiques, on the subway, at cocktail parties, and inside fashionable nightclubs and regale them with jokes and anecdotes. (If you're that type of person.)

And if you're thinking, All right. It's only a quiz book, it's not the Gettysburg Address—wait! There's more. Because, like the artist himself, *Fun with Woody* has its introspective side. Supplementing over five hundred informative questions, is a provocative series of lively, insightful quotes from Woody himself (as well as others)—culled from twenty-three years of interviews with newspapers, magazines, and biographers—that provide an intriguing look into how Woody has regarded the evolution of his art.

You'll learn what was really autobiographical about *Annie Hall* . . . why Woody respects the craft of screenwriting about as much as he respects college professors . . . and why he admits his first serious drama, *Interiors*, was less than successful.

Maybe what you really care about are priceless facts like how many women Woody has dated onscreen . . . what Woody Allen character came on too strong for a nymphomaniac . . . and which leading psychologist proved that "death is an acquired trait."

Whatever your preference, I hope you'll find this Woody Allen primer as entertaining to read as it is to answer. However you choose to read the book—whether sequentially or by picking chapters at random—your knowledge of Woody is sure to increase dramatically by the time you finish. You may also become funnier, more neurotic, and completely ill at ease with machines—but I won't take credit for that.

Read and learn, laugh and enjoy. It's time to have Fun with Woody.

—Graham Flashner,
November 1987

FUN WITH WOODY

EARLY DAYS

"I was shy, and everything *dissatisfied me, although I didn't know why. I had this intense sense of failure. But although I never laughed out loud then, I was a funny kid. My viewpoint was funny, and I said funny things."*
— The New York Times Magazine, *1963*

"For the first fifteen years of my life I never read. I was just interested in going out in the street and playing ball."
—Newsweek, *1978*

1. Woody Allen was born in the Flatbush section of Brooklyn on
   a. November 23, 1933
   b. December 1, 1935
   c. June 6, 1935
   d. April 7, 1935

2. Woody Allen's real name (at least, the public version) is
   a. Allen Stewart Konigsberg
   b. Adam Steven Greenberg
   c. Stewart Allan Guttenberg
   d. Sidney Michael Shatzenbergger

3. Woody's parents, whose values he would later joke are "God and carpeting," are named
   a. Stanley and Ethel
   b. Howie and Sophie
   c. Sol and Louise
   d. Martin and Nettie

"He was all schoolyard. They threw him a football once, he tried to dribble it."
—Description of Alvy Singer's athletic prowess, from Annie Hall

4. Contrary to his image, Woody was actually a good athlete while growing up. "Sports is everything theater should be," Woody once said, and growing up in Brooklyn, he played almost every sport imaginable, *except*
   a. stickball
   b. basketball
   c. field hockey
   d. tennis

"Even while I was reading nothing but Donald Duck and Batman I could write real prose in school compositions. There was never a week when the composition I wrote was not the one that was to be read to the class."   —Newsweek, *1978*

5. Woody did attend high school ("a gruesome experience," he notes) in Brooklyn. Which one?
   a. Central High
   b. Franklin High
   c. Midwood High
   d. Flatbush High

6. Woody was hardly enamored of college. As he recalled in an interview, as often as not he would stay on the train, skip the

stop where his college was, and go to the movies. By now, everyone should know that Woody was indeed booted out of
    a. Fordham and Brooklyn College
    b. Manhattan College and Hunter
    c. St. John's and Pace University
    d. NYU and City College

7. TRUE OR FALSE: Woody Allen is not an only child.

*"At that time the minimum wage you got working for a tailor
or something was seventy-five cents an hour. I'd give them fifty
jokes a day. There was nothing to it. I'd get out of school, get on
the BMT subway, and start listing jokes. Always five to a page,
ten pages."* —The New York Times Magazine, *1963*

8. Woody's quips were being devoured by local press agents, and
fed into the hands of comedians. Eventually, Woody was hired
by one such public relations firm at twenty-five dollars a week
for twenty hours of work. The firm was
    a. Mahoney/Wasserman Associates
    b. Nancy Seltzer and Associates
    c. Siegelman and Morton Associates
    d. David O. Alber Associates

*"He would come in from Brooklyn every afternoon, and in three
hours turn out thirty or forty absolutely marvelous jokes, then
pick up his schoolbooks and go home."*
               —Colleague at Woody's P.R. firm, *1963*

9. After his gag-writing experience, not to mention an uncere-
monious firing from "The Garry Moore Show," Woody enrolled
in a Writers Development Program at
    a. NBC
    b. CBS

c. ABC
d. PBS

10. Woody's big television break came with a TV special he collaborated on for Sid Caesar, Art Carney, and Shirley MacLaine, which was nominated for an Emmy. Who was Woody's collaborator?
   a. Larry Gelbart
   b. Mel Brooks
   c. Neil Simon
   d. Mike Nichols

11. Dissatisfied with writing jokes for others, Woody, galvanized by the performances of Mort Sahl, and goaded by his agents/managers Jack Rollins and Charles Joffe, decided to give up his anonymity and step out onstage to perform his own material. He debuted late in 1960 in New York, at which club?
   a. the hungry i
   b. the Bitter End
   c. the Duplex
   d. the Village Gate

"I wrote more specials for Sid and Art, but I had no real interest in TV writing after I got over the glamour. I wanted to be a playwright. I kept going to the theater and reading books. Then a funny thing happened; I began to come up with comedy ideas that could only be expressed in monologues."
—In Eric Lax, On Being Funny: Woody Allen and Comedy, *1975*

12. Who was the Broadway producer responsible for bringing *Don't Drink the Water*, Woody's first play, to the stage?
   a. Max Gordon
   b. David Merrick
   c. Samuel Goldwyn
   d. Hal Prince

13. TRUE OR FALSE: Woody has been managed throughout his entire career by Jack Rollins and Charles Joffe.

"I'm a compulsive rewriter. I usually do half a dozen drafts. When I've shot a film and I'm working on it in the editing room, then I work the other way. . . . I work very, very slowly and very meticulously so that the first cut is quite close to the film that comes out. I could almost show my first cut to an audience."
—Saturday Review, *1980*

14. Woody Allen's first break into the movies came when
   a. producer Charles Feldman ran into him one night eating the Warren Beatty sandwich at the Carnegie Deli
   b. Feldman read one of Woody's short stories and phoned his agent immediately
   c. Feldman, along with Shirley MacLaine, saw Woody in performance at the Blue Angel
   d. Feldman decided Woody was the perfect actor for a sex comedy he had in mind about a Jewish neurotic who can't get laid

15. Woody's script for *Take the Money and Run* was wanted by a number of studios, but Rollins and Joffe insisted that Woody be allowed to act in it and make his directorial debut as well. At one point, United Artists wanted to buy it, provided the film could be shot for $750,000—a budget deemed impossible by everyone concerned. (The film was shot for $1.6 million.) Which studio finally bought the script?
   a. Warner Brothers
   b. 20th Century–Fox
   c. Palomar Pictures
   d. Columbia Pictures

16. Woody has created an extremely distinct set of character names for himself in his films. Match the character name with the movie Woody plays him in:

The Bitter End in Greenwich Village,
one of Woody's early stand-up haunts.
Courtesy of Todd Lane

1. Isaac Davis
2. Fielding Mellish
3. Victor Shakopopolis
4. Boris Grushenko
5. Miles Monroe
6. Virgil Starkwell
7. Mickey Sachs

a. *Sleeper*
b. *Love and Death*
c. *Take the Money and Run*
d. *Manhattan*
e. *Everything You Always Wanted to Know About Sex . . .*
f. *Hannah and Her Sisters*
g. *Bananas*

"The schlemiel image never did describe me. . . . I've never been that. It's an appellation for the unimaginative to hang on me. The things I did on nightclub stages were fantasies or exaggerations from my own life—school, women, parents—which I set out in an amusing way." —Newsweek, *1978*

2

THE NIGHTCLUB YEARS
Stand-up Woody

"It was unspeakably agonizing. I didn't know what I was doing. All day long, I would shake and tremble, thinking about standing up that night before people and trying to be funny."

—Seventeen, *1975*

Complete the Quote

Q1. "It so happens, that on my honeymoon night, my wife stopped in the middle of everything to give me a _____."

Q2. "Sex is a beautiful thing between two people. Between _____ it's fantastic!"

Q3. "In an effort . . . to prolong the moment of ecstasy . . . I think of _____."

Q4. "I asked her if she would commit adultery with me . . . told her it was nothing personal. She said, 'Not even . . . if it would help _____.' "

Q5. "The maharaja's daughter was so taken with my heroism . . . she gave me . . . a mammoth . . . _____."

"Onstage, he is a little less slender than the microphone, which he frequently seems to lean on for support."
—The New York Times Magazine, *1963*

"I worked at my own expense, financially and emotionally, going down to some God-forsaken, mostly empty club at 11:00 P.M. and then nobody would laugh. I wanted to die. But gradually, the act caught on." —The New York Times Magazine, *1963*

17. In one routine, after shooting a moose, Woody realizes he's in trouble when it wakes up in the Holland Tunnel. He takes it to a costume party, introducing the moose as the Solomons. "The moose mingles," Woody reports. "Did very well. Scored." How?
a. He made love to the Berkowitzes.
b. Some guy was trying to sell him insurance for an hour and a half.
c. Some woman was trying to sell him futures.
d. A couple dressed as a moose made love to him.

18. "The Berkowitzes are shot, stuffed, and mounted, at _____. And the joke's on them 'cause it's restricted!"
a. the New York Athletic Club
b. the Elks Club
c. the Rotary Club
d. the New York Polo Club

19. Woody is kidnapped. FBI agents surround the house, telling the kidnappers they can "keep the kid" when the kidnappers state a preference for holding on to their guns. How do the FBI agents finally induce the kidnappers to surrender?
a. They lob laughing gas into the house.
b. They lob tear gas into the house.
c. They pose as an immense charm bracelet.
d. They put on the death scene from *Camille.*

20. According to Woody, his parents did not want him as a child, going so far as to put _____ in his crib.
   a. a grenade
   b. a pet rat
   c. a live teddy bear
   d. a "rattle" snake

21. Why did Woody claim to identify at an early age with Superman?
   a. They both liked to use X-ray vision on female bodies.
   b. They both liked to leap tall buildings.
   c. They both liked to remove their clothes in phone booths.
   d. They both wore the same kind of glasses as Clark Kent.

22. Woody claims that *What's New, Pussycat?* was not his first acting role. In nursery school, he won accolades for his portrayal of
   a. Homer
   b. Biff Loman
   c. Tevye
   d. Stanley Kowalski

23. After Woody is aced out for a date with a European girl, she brings along a sister for Woody—Sister Mary Teresa. "We discussed the New Testament," Woody reports. "We agreed that *He* was well adjusted for an only child." Who aced Woody out for the first girl?
   a. Peter O'Toole
   b. Billy Graham
   c. Warren Beatty
   d. James Bond

24. While still in Europe, Woody claims to play vibes. Why?
   a. It helps him come on to a parrot.
   b. It helps him sublimate his sexual tensions.
   c. It will make him live longer.
   d. It helps him massage his vital organs.

25. Reminiscing about his time spent with Ernest Hemingway, Woody recalls Scott and Zelda coming back from their "wild New Year's party." What was unusual about this party?
  a. It was really Armistice Day.
  b. No one else attended.
  c. There was no food or beverage.
  d. It took place in April.

26. Woody says that when Smirnoff called Woody to do a vodka ad with Monique van Doren (yes, there really was such an ad), he jokes that they wanted Noël Coward first, but he was busy
  a. removing the dialogue from *The Trojan Women*
  b. removing the music and lyrics from *My Fair Lady*
  c. removing the music from *West Side Story*
  d. posing for Jack Daniel's with Twiggy

27. According to the routine, who eventually wound up posing with Monique, after advising Woody not to do it, even though it paid $50,000?
  a. his mother
  b. his analyst
  c. his lawyer
  d. his rabbi

28. "My body will not tolerate spirits," Woody recalls. "I drank two martinis on New Year's Eve and tried to
  a. pull my pants over my head"
  b. compete at the Preakness"
  c. hijack an elevator and fly it to Cuba"
  d. dance a *pas de deux* on top of an anvil"

"She was a philosophy major at Hunter College, so I had four years of philosophy with her by proxy. She got me out of my parents' house; I had to earn a living and deal with real-life problems." —On his first marriage, to Harlene Rosen

COME OUT OF YOUR SHELL...TRY SMIRNOFF

One of Woody Allen's vodka ads for Smirnoff.
Courtesy of Richard Daley Studios

. . .

Woody married Harlene at nineteen (she was sixteen). He later
described the split-up as a basic difference in direction (in the
routine, he refers to the marriage as "The Ox-Bow Incident").
They had basic differences over Woody's satirical humor as well,
resulting in a million-dollar lawsuit for defamation of character
(eventually settled out of court), possibly for jokes like the following:

29. "She was coming home late at night and she was violated . . . that's what the papers said the next day. They asked
me to comment, and I said, 'Knowing my wife,
   a. she only violated herself' "
   b. it was not a moving violation' "
   c. it was not a parking violation' "
   d. it was not a paid violation' "

30. In addition to calling her one of the few White Muslims in
New York, Woody also jokes about running into her and not
recognizing her with
   a. her mouth closed
   b. her blouse closed
   c. her wrists closed
   d. her face level

31. Match the fictional character from Woody's routines to the
correct action or description:

1. Sheldon Finkelstein	a. had biggest overbite in Brooklyn
2. Guy de Maupassant Rabinowitz	b. stepped on Spot, Woody's ant
3. Woody's cousin	c. Woody attended his birthday party
4. Hermina Jaffe	
5. Floyd	

That's Woody Allen behind those Foster Grants. *Courtesy of Foster Grant Corp.*

6. Seymour Gutkin
7. Leo

d. beat Woody's violin into his leg
e. parents voted for Hitler in the Dewey-Roosevelt election
f. wife had orgasmic insurance from Mutual of Omaha
g. part Mexican, part nonfat dry milk

"I did not like elementary school, or high school, and I liked college the least of the three. I was working, and I was impatient to be working even more."

—The New York Times Magazine, *1963*

32. Woody claims to have been a _____ major at NYU.
   a. history of oral sex
   b. history of periodontics
   c. history of hygiene
   d. history of reptile sex

33. Woody says he was tossed out of NYU for looking within the
soul of the boy sitting next to him on his metaphysics final. At
City College, he jokes, he was also thrown out for cheating, this
time
   a. with the dean's wife
   b. on an existentialism test that no one took
   c. with the entire faculty of the psych department
   d. on an optometrist's eye chart

34. What was Woody's mother's supposed reaction to his flunking
out of two colleges?

a. She locked herself in the furnace.
b. She took an overdose of Mah-Jongg tiles.
c. She swallowed a cup of Drano.
d. She burned her Bible.

35. Woody fell in love for the first time in his freshman year, but did not marry the girl, he notes sadly, because
a. he was a Jew, she was an Arab, and they had a personal Six-Day War
b. they were both agnostics, and didn't know whether to believe in marriage
c. she could not marry any man under six feet
d. he was an atheist, she was an agnostic, and they couldn't figure out which religion not to bring the children up in

36. In one routine, Woody bemoans his few experiences with blind dates, noting that the last one was
a. an undercover narcotics officer who overdosed on heroin
b. beaten up by Mafia hoods as they sat in a restaurant in Chinatown
c. carted away to Bellevue by two men in white jackets with a butterfly net
d. arrested by Israeli agents as they sat at the Stork Club

37. Woody does not consider himself a swinger. His idea of a swinging night out is to
a. watch the paint dry on a newly painted house
b. lie down under a cloudless sky and search for the Milky Way
c. count the number of grains of sand at the beach
d. watch the chickens revolve at the corner rotisserie

38. Woody broke two teeth giving a hickey to the Statue of Liberty after
a. swallowing two sugar cubes
b. inhaling next to an Armenian
c. imbibing two quarts of electric Kool-Aid
d. taking a puff on the wrong cigarette

39. Woody's mistrust of mechanical objects is legendary. Fill in the defects of the following:

(i) a clock that runs _____

(ii) a tape recorder that says _____

(iii) a sun lamp that _____

40. After beating up his television set, Woody gets his come-uppance from _____ that makes an anti-Semitic remark after terrifying him.

    a. a revolving door

    b. a swivel chair

    c. an elevator

    d. a stairwell

41. Though poor, Woody's parents decide to buy him a pet. They take him to the Damaged Pet Shop, where he gets

    a. a straight camel

    b. a bent pussycat

    c. a dog that stutters

    d. a midget giraffe

42. Finally, Woody gets married, by a reformed rabbi. "A *very* reformed rabbi," he notes. "A _____."

    a. KKK Grand Dragon

    b. Nazi

    c. Frenchman

    d. Negro

43. Woody is hired at an advertising agency to be their "show Jew," to prove they can work with minorities. But eventually, he is fired, for

    a. taking off too many Jewish holidays

    b. reading his memos right to left

    c. working with a menorah on his desk

    d. going home early on Friday nights

44. Woody's house is surrounded, in SWAT-team fashion, by the staff of the New York Public Library, demanding their overdue books. The library punishes him by

a. putting him on its Ten-Most-Wanted List, with his face
   hung on a poster in Barnes & Noble
b. spanking him with Webster's Dictionary
c. tailing him relentlessly with a mousy librarian, who
   blows a whistle every time he picks up a book
d. taking away his glasses for a year

45. When Woody comes home to tell his parents he's just gotten
divorced, his mother is knitting a chicken, while Dad is
   a. sitting on an air hose
   b. watching the Indiana Home for the Criminally Insane
      Glee Club on TV
   c. trying to play "Flight of the Bumblebee" on his tuba
   d. reading bedtime stories to a Cornish hen

*"I suppose my humor appeals to people because I look at things
differently. My reactions to everyday situations seem normal to
me, but completely hilarious to everyone else, and most of the
time I can't figure out why."*
                              —The New York Times Magazine, *1963*

3

WHAT'S NEW, PUSSYCAT?

"I wrote an offbeat script about a hypersexual guy living in Paris and afraid to get married. Establishment people poured money into it. While they managed to retain some of the jokes, they lost 50 percent of them."   —Seventeen, *1972*

46. TRUE OR FALSE: The title of the movie refers to the greeting Warren Beatty gave women when he called them on the telephone.

"I saw the picture once, fleetingly, years ago. I don't remember much about it at all. I certainly don't remember any of the dialogue. A lot of ad-libbing went on, which I like in the films I direct, but there was nobody on Pussycat *to control the ad-libbing. They just slopped it all on the screen."*   —Cinema, *1972*

47. What is Woody Allen, as Victor Shakopopolis, doing when we first see him onscreen?

    a. dressing a stripper backstage at her show
    b. being analyzed by Dr. Fritz Fassbender

    c. playing (and cheating at) chess at an outdoor café
    d. trying to pick up a woman in a bordello

48. According to himself, when does Michael James (Peter O'Toole) become "almost handsome"?
    a. when his face is reflected through a prism
    b. when he stands upside down during an eclipse
    c. when he sits under a fluorescent light
    d. when the light hits him in a certain direction

49. Who bumps into Michael at the Crazy Horse Saloon, asking him, "Haven't you seen me somewhere before?"
    a. Warren Beatty
    b. Richard Burton
    c. Charlton Heston
    d. Alec Guinness

50. At one point in the movie, the words *Author's Message* are flashed on the screen, while Michael rambles on about
    a. the need to be as sexually fulfilled as possible before marriage
    b. the need to forsake superficial affairs for true love
    c. the need to keep being sexually fulfilled after marriage
    d. the need to forsake true love for one-night stands with unattainable women

51. What does Victor say after trying to kiss Carol (Romy Schneider) for the first time?
    a. "I saw your lips standing there."
    b. "My lips were hungry."
    c. "Your lips were in the way"
    d. "I thought my lips were chapped."

52. According to Liz Bien (Paula Prentiss), the poem she reads to an impatient Michael entitled "Ode to a Pacifist Junkie" is
    a. a diatribe against LSD
    b. a plea for better housing
    c. a story of birth control during the Restoration
    d. an ode to an antiwar heroin addict

Michael James and Dr. Fritz Fassbender
(Peter Sellers) contemplate their "problems" with women.
Courtesy of United Artists Pictures, Inc.

Victor Shakopopolis attempts to keep his mind on
chess. *Courtesy of United Artists Pictures, Inc.*

53. When does Renée Lefebvre (Capucine) blow the whistle that she wears around her neck?
   a. when she calls her dog for dinner
   b. when she sees a sexy man she likes
   c. when she has trouble controlling herself
   d. while she is on-duty as a traffic cop

54. When does Carol decide to move into Michael's apartment?
   a. while Renée Lefebvre is in another room, canceling an appointment so she can stay the night
   b. after Victor tries to make love to her on top of the Eiffel Tower
   c. after Michael threatens to tell her parents she's not been faithful
   d. She never tries to move in.

55. While eating a midnight dinner on the banks of the Seine, Victor decides to be psychoanalyzed by Dr. Fritz, interrupting him at
   a. masturbation
   b. lovemaking
   c. a temper tantrum
   d. a suicide attempt

56. The character said by Fritz to be "a personal friend of James Bond" is played by
   a. Romy Schneider
   b. Capucine
   c. Peter O'Toole
   d. Ursula Andress

57. In Woody's original ending for the film, his character, Victor, wins Carol away from the hesitant Michael. Producer Charles Feldman resisted this, and had Carol and Michael marry because
   a. he was an old-fashioned believer in marriage
   b. of box-office concerns; Peter O'Toole was a much better draw than Woody Allen at the time

c. he and Woody argued so vociferously over the script he decided not to let him get the girl

d. Victor was perceived as an aimless bum, unworthy of a woman like Carol

58. How does Ursula Andress make her first appearance in the film?

a. She seduces Fritz at a Halloween party dressed as a pussycat.

b. She parachutes inadvertently into Michael's car.

c. She's in Victor's bed when he wakes from a nap.

d. She's seen in a bikini on a French billboard for tanning cream.

59. What is the name of the hotel that all the film's main characters wind up vacationing at, in the film's madcap finale?

a. the Ritz Carlton

b. Château Plato

c. Château Chantel

d. Cupid Inn

60. Trying to seduce a girl in his hotel room, Victor sets a romantic mood by

a. lip-syncing to opera

b. adorning the bed with candles

c. reciting Rimbaud while pulling off her clothes

d. creating a fake scene of a sunset and mist in the room

"I fought with everybody all the time. I hated everyone, and everyone hated me. When that picture was over I decided I would never do another film unless I had complete control of it."

—Cinema, *1972*

4

WHAT'S UP, TIGER LILY?

"We all got into a locked room together. We kept running loops all day long for weeks, and writing the story, making it up as we went along. And it turned out that what we really wanted was more dialogue, and the film would sag when there was less. But we didn't know that at first. We did it, and I turned it over to the producer."
—Cinema, *1972*

61. What is the original title of the Japanese spy film the movie is based on?
   a. *The Seven Samurai*
   b. *Key of Keys*
   c. *You Only Die Twice*
   d. *Warrior Women*

62. TRUE OR FALSE: The producers at American International Pictures originally were set to release the film with the same title and appropriate English subtitles.

"All we did was put five people in a room and keep them there improvising as the film ran. It was a nuisance but OK. We still haven't seen any money from it, though. —Rolling Stone, *1971*

...

*T*he Japanese film, which appeared on the heels of the latest James Bond release *Goldfinger*, attempted to satirize every aspect of the Bond phenomenon. Woody replaced the original story line with one depicting a manic search for a recipe for the world's best egg salad. He also transformed the main character from an Oriental superspy into an Occidental nebbish.

...

63. A mysterious young woman, clad only in a bath towel, opens it alluringly to a breathless Phil Moskowitz. She then asks him to
   a. taper her robe
   b. wear her earrings
   c. name three presidents
   d. name the shortstop for the 1964 St. Louis Cardinals

64. Who exclaims, "I was almost shot and killed before the opening credits"?
   a. Shepherd Wong
   b. Wing Fat
   c. Woody Allen
   d. Phil Moskowitz

65. Before the film begins, Woody, explaining how he redubbed the soundtrack, notes that this is not the first time Japanese actors were dubbed by American voices. It also happened, he claims, in
   a. *Gone With the Wind*
   b. *The Sound of Music*
   c. *The Seven Year Itch*
   d. *Casino Royale*

66. The producer of the movie, Henry Saperstein (whom Woody later sued for tampering with his work), was worried enough about the movie's commercial potential to insert a popular Amer-

ican rock band into the original movie footage, completely unrelated to the plot. In this way, he hoped to appeal to young rock
viewers. Who was the featured band?

a. The Grateful Dead
b. Jefferson Airplane
c. The Lovin' Spoonful
d. Peter, Paul, and Mary

67. The last time Wing Fat made love on a ship, why didn't he
finish?

a. He was on the *Lusitania*, being torpedoed by Germans.
b. He was on the *Titanic*.
c. His lover left him to watch the *Hindenburg*.
d. He got seasick and threw up during foreplay.

68. What is so "special" about Phil's camera?

a. It can impregnate a woman while taking her picture.
b. It emits a laser beam that can destroy Japan.
c. Everyone photographed comes out naked.
d. It can transform all objects into hairpieces.

69. As Shepherd Wong is dying, he makes a last request. Rather
than being embalmed, he wants to be

a. stuffed with crabmeat
b. cremated on the outside
c. buried next to James Bond
d. taken to the New York World's Fair

70. Late in the movie, a villain tortures Phil and the Yaki sisters,
who are all tied to a chair, by

a. scraping a piece of chalk across a blackboard
b. performing ventriloquism with live lobsters
c. doing a Peter Lorre imitation
d. singing Maurice Chevalier's greatest hits

71. At one point, a warden addressing the prisoners over a loud-
speaker says, "We'll have more reasons why you'll never get

away, but first, here's Len Maxwell with the weather." Len Maxwell is

  a. the warden's lover
  b. Phil Moskowitz's Oriental name
  c. one of the voices on the movie's soundtrack
  d. owner of Maxwell House coffee

72. "Shut the door, I'm naked." Who says this?
  a. Terry Yaki
  b. Louise Lasser, in the projection room with Woody Allen
  c. a chicken about to be devoured by a cobra
  d. a recorded voice in Shepherd Wong's safe

73. In the last shot of the film, Phil Moskowitz, instead of going
off with the two sisters, has retreated into fantasy, thinking he's
  a. The Man from U.N.C.L.E.
  b. Emperor Hirohito
  c. a Pan Am jet
  d. Ursula Andress

74. *Visually*, what is a young Oriental girl doing when she notes,
"Boy, am I a piece"?
  a. calisthenics
  b. cooking dumplings
  c. making love
  d. taking hemorrhoid pills

75. After he sees his mother in a line of call girls aboard a ship,
what is Wing Fat's reaction?
  a. He seduces her, at a discount rate.
  b. He punches her.
  c. He throws her overboard.
  d. He jumps overboard in shame.

76. At one point, Phil invokes a famous scene from *Peter Pan*,
imploring the audience to clap so he can
  a. get it up and sleep with Suzi Yaki
  b. eat up Shepherd Wong's entire supply of egg salad

    c. get his gun reloaded in order to shoot three assassins
    d. get support for a Best Actor nomination

77. "Thank you for clearing up my sinuses." Terry Yaki says this to Phil after
    a. he gives her egg salad
    b. he makes love to her
    c. he spanks her with a jar of Hellmann's
    d. he blows her nose

5

CASINO ROYALE

"Last winter, producer Charles K. Feldman approached me to appear in his new James Bond extravaganza, Casino Royale— *not, as I had expected, as James Bond, but as 007's nephew, Little Jimmy Bond . . . we dickered for a few days, until I asked him if there were going to be any girls in the picture. He started listing them, and three hours later I interrupted to accept his original cash offer of three dollars."* —Playboy, *1967*

78. The first time we see Jimmy Bond, he is about to be executed in
  a. South America
  b. Manhattan
  c. Borneo
  d. New Delhi

79. In an execution scene that Woody ad-libbed, Jimmy Bond escapes the firing squad by
  a. fleeing while his double appears to absorb the bullets
  b. tossing an exploding cigarette at his executioners and climbing over a wall

c. being pulled up to safety by a SMERSH helicopter just as the executioners open fire
d. telling a frantic series of jokes that leave his execution-ers helpless with laughter, letting Jimmy turn the tables and execute *them*

"I wrote the last part of the script, my part, and at first they said it went in a different direction from the rest of the script. Three months later, they wrote and asked me if I had a carbon of the pages I'd sent them because they were heading in my di-rection and would reshape the whole script to fit it."
—Seventeen, *1972*

80. *Casino Royale*'s out-of-control production excess may only have been exceeded by its script revisions. The final credits be-longed to Wolf Mankowitz, John Law, and Michael Sayers, but half the Writers Guild probably worked on it in some form or another, while Woody Allen was kept on hand by Feldman in London for nearly six months of idleness (during which time *Don't Drink the Water* was written). Why, then is Woody's name not on the final credits?
a. Woody lost a Writers Guild arbitration, which decreed that he had written too insignificant a portion of the film.
b. In a fit of anger, Feldman yanked Woody's name from the credits after a long argument.
c. None of Woody's scenes appeared in the final version.
d. Woody himself made sure Feldman left his name off, as he was disgusted by the final result.

"I ad-libbed lines of my own. I didn't even know what was going on. They paid me a lot of money, wasted a lot of time for ages. I sat around in London for about five and a half months waiting to shoot."
—Cinema, *1972*

81. After Jimmy's brief first appearance, we don't see him again until the film's closing segment, when we find out he is the evil Dr. Noah, head of SMERSH, and ready to conquer the world with his bacillus, which
    a. makes all women blond and destroys all men with over-bites
    b. makes all women 5'6" and destroys all men who like other men
    c. makes all women beautiful and destroys all men over 4'6"
    d. makes all women orgasmic and destroys all men under 4'6"

82. In the lascivious picture on page 33, Jimmy has The Detainer (Daliah Lavi) strapped to a torture bed with aluminum bonds. What is his explanation of why he's done this?
    a. He always ties up girls he has a crush on.
    b. He learned it in the Boy Scouts.
    c. He is satisfying her most lurid sexual fantasy.
    d. He must extract spy secrets from cathodes hidden inside the bonds.

83. When is Jimmy Bond's birthday?
    a. Bastille Day
    b. New Year's Eve
    c. Good Friday
    d. April Fool's Day

84. When he finally confronts his Uncle James, Jimmy is at last cured of his chronic
    a. impotence
    b. catatonia
    c. speechlessness
    d. hemorrhoids

85. What is Jimmy's master plan which will enable him to rule the world in five days?
    a. All world leaders will be assassinated and replaced by doubles under his control.

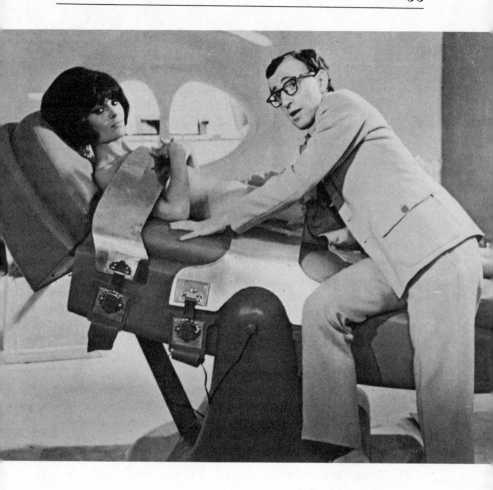

Woody with Daliah Lavi.
Courtesy of Columbia Pictures

b. A secret drug will render the world's population three
feet tall and blind.

c. All women will be replaced by doubles who will have
eyes only for Jimmy.

d. none of the above

86. Jimmy eventually blows up the entire proceedings in a madcap
casino climax that took two months and some $1 million to shoot.
He does this after swallowing

a. an entire bottle of nitroglycerin and smoking a cigarette

b. four hundred tiny time pills that leave him a walking
atomic bomb

c. two hundred tablets of plutonium that detonate upon
contact with the body

d. a massive dose of Ex-Lax mixed with sulfur dioxide

87. At one point in the movie, a brief refrain of the title song
from *What's New, Pussycat?* is heard when

a. Mati Bond (Joanna Pettet) opens up a manhole cover

b. the real 007 hallucinates at a wild military orgy

c. Vesper Lynd pulls back her shower curtain

d. Jimmy Bond kisses The Detainer

88. In another nod to *What's New, Pussycat?* Peter O'Toole, who
came to the set just to say hello, ended up in a cameo in the
"Highlanders" sequence (in a take he thought was a rehearsal)
asking Evelyn Tremble (Peter Sellers) if he's

a. Montgomery Clift

b. Fritz Fassbender

c. Richard Burton

d. Frank Sinatra

89. *Casino Royale* provides an early foreshadowing of Woody
Allen characters' incompetence with machines. Here, Jimmy Bond

a. gets trapped in The Detainer's aluminum bonds

b. is pressed by a steam iron

c. locks himself in an automatic dryer

d. falls off a mechanical rocking horse

Woody displays his famed bacillus
to David Niven and Joanna Pettet.
Courtesy of Columbia Pictures

90. Who says, "This gun shoots backwards—I've just killed my-self"?
    a. Orson Welles
    b. Jean-Paul Belmondo
    c. William Holden
    d. George Raft

91. Late in the movie, little Jimmy is rendered helpless when his glasses are knocked off. What is Evelyn Tremble's explanation of why *he* wears glasses?
    a. "I like to see who I'm shooting."
    b. "I like to see who I'm screwing."
    c. "I like to see how I'm cheating."
    d. "No one ever told me not to."

92. Who described *Casino Royale* as an "unredeemingly moronic enterprise; a handbook on how not to make a film"?
    a. Pauline Kael
    b. Sean Connery
    c. John Huston
    d. Woody Allen

"I never bothered to see the film. It was a chaotic madhouse. . . . I knew then that the only way to make films is to control them completely."   —Cinema, *1972*

6

THE PLAY'S THE THING
Woody in the Theater

DON'T DRINK THE WATER

"I didn't know anything about writing a play, but I wrote it. We made twelve fast changes—the most in history for a straight play out of town—and fired the director. I was sick with a 102° temperature. It was utter bedlam; the play was going down the drain. But when it finally opened in New York it was undeniably funny."
—*Commenting on* Don't Drink the Water, Harper's Bazaar, *1971*

93. "This embassy is United States territory," says the hapless Axel Magee indignantly to the secret police agent, Krojack. "Nobody can be _____ without the written consent of the American government."
    a. forced to strip
    b. sprayed with a fire extinguisher
    c. dragged away and shot
    d. labeled an Ugly American

94. According to Father Drobney, the ambassador's son, Axel Magee, is the only man in the history of the foreign service to

Woody in rehearsals
with Danny Aiello and
Beatrice Arthur for
*The Floating Light
Bulb. Courtesy of AP/
Wide World Photos*

    a. be unable to differentiate between a Russian and a plate
       of herring
    b. accidentally wrap his lunch in a peace treaty
    c. be fired from eighteen different embassies on the same
       day
    d. sublease rooms in the embassy to Third World arms
       dealers

95. What is the name of the fictional country in which *Don't Drink
the Water* takes place?
    a. South Germany
    b. Flumania
    c. Vulgaria
    d. Dungary

96. Walter Hollander is a caterer who takes tremendous pride in
his work. As he recounts, his company was the first to make
    a. bar-mitzvah boys out of bratwurst
    b. choirboys out of rice pudding
    c. cadavers out of tortilla chips
    d. bridegrooms out of potato salad

97. What is Walter's explanation of why he won't sleep on a cot
in the embassy?

    a. "I cannot sleep on anything that might have been used in the army."
    b. "I'm a caterer; I've made cots out of linguini."
    c. "I refuse to make love on anything without a headboard."
    d. "I'm a dignified man with a hernia."

98. Walter's beautiful daughter Susan, who is backing out of her marriage plans thanks to her burgeoning romance with Axel, has almost married three different guys. They were
    a. a sex pervert, a bank robber, and an exterminator
    b. a heavy-metal guitarist, an acid head, and a castrated Mafia boss
    c. a manic-depressive jazz musician, a draft dodger, and a defrocked priest
    d. a KGB agent, a blind race driver, and a toilet-seat manufacturer

99. Woody Allen did not participate in the film version of *Don't Drink the Water*, directed by Howard Morris, because
    a. no one asked him to
    b. he had no desire to adapt it to the screen; he was quoted as saying that he was sure it wouldn't work
    c. director Howard Morris refused to let him play the part of Axel Magee
    d. the screenwriters, R. S. Allen and Harvey Bullock, wrote such a sensational screenplay that Woody decided they might as well use that

THE ONE-ACTS

100. Three of Woody's one-act plays (*God, Death,* and *Sex*) were to be produced during the 1973–74 Broadway season. They weren't, and remain confined to his collections. *God* and *Death* appear in Woody's book *Without Feathers*, which was published in 1975. *Sex* has not appeared anywhere in print. Why weren't the shows ever produced?

   a. No Broadway producer thought them commercial enough.

   b. Woody wanted to act in all three, but was too busy making *Sleeper*.

   c. Because of the elaborate sets, the plays would have cost $250,000 to produce—too much to make a profit.

   d. They were all set to go when a strike by Actors Equity crippled Broadway for six months.

101. What is Kleinman's part in the "plan," organized by neighborhood vigilantes to catch the murderer in *Death*?

   a. He is to dress up like Zsa Zsa Gabor and lie down, coughing, in the middle of the street.

   b. He is to hop up and down, yodeling, as soon as a searchlight hits him.

   c. As he is suspected of being the killer, the vigilantes are going to set him up with two luscious young women and see what he does with them.

   d. He is never told about the plan.

102. Anna, Kleinman's wife, arouses his skepticism when she tells how *she* would ward off the attacker, if he broke into the house, by

   a. blowing pepper in his eyes

   b. singing "Yankee Doodle Dandy" backward at high volume

   c. shampooing his gun

   d. breaking his kneecap with the toilet plunger

103. TRUE OR FALSE: Hans Spiro, the telepathist, deduces that Kleinman is the murderer after correctly guessing what Kleinman had for dinner a week ago Tuesday.

104. Though the characters in *God* talk with decidedly modern inflections, the play is actually set in

   a. Rome, A.D. 1000

   b. Athens, 500 B.C.

   c. Jerusalem, A.D. 300

   d. North Africa, 700 B.C.

105. At one point, Diabetes, the actor, calls up an unseen Woody Allen (the writer of the play the audience is watching) to talk about a strange girl, Doris Levine, who has appeared onstage. Diabetes uses a line to describe her that Woody says he used later in *Play It Again, Sam*. He describes her as
   a. a New York left-wing Jewish intellectual with a nose job
   b. a nymphomaniac with the I.Q. of a lobster
   c. a typical product of the Brooklyn College cafeteria
   d. a typical result of a broken home

106. The character Trichinosis has just come from a discussion with Socrates at the Acropolis, where Socrates upset him by
   a. proving he didn't exist
   b. requesting that he pull his pants down while people were watching
   c. renouncing the Greek language as ancient
   d. asking him to swallow hemlock

107. Once she has realized that the universe, life, and the characters onstage are meaningless, Doris Levine blurts out that she has a "sudden and overpowering urge" to
   a. dance naked in front of relatives
   b. swallow LSD
   c. imitate a dog
   d. get laid

108. At the conclusion of the play, a Western Union messenger arrives with a telegram, which is Woody's message to his characters. It states that
   a. God is alive, and Hepatitis will never write for the theater again
   b. God is dead, and Doris Levine can definitely have an orgasm, if she wants
   c. God is dead, and Woody is going to enjoy an orgasm with Blanche DuBois
   d. God is alive, and any doubters in the audience should please see the usher in Section 4

109. *Death Knocks* parodies Ingmar Bergman's *The Seventh Seal*, in which a knight plays chess with Death and keeps him at bay long enough to roam the countryside searching for Answers. In *Death Knocks*, Nat Ackerman is visited by Death, but happily postpones his final farewell by beating Death at
  a. badminton
  b. poker
  c. hearts
  d. gin rummy

110. Ackerman is disappointed by Death's physical appearance because
  a. he doesn't look like Mickey Mantle
  b. he looks like Ackerman
  c. he looks very cold
  d. he looks effeminate

111. TRUE OR FALSE: Not only does Death wind up losing to Ackerman, but he also owes him twenty-eight dollars.

THE FLOATING LIGHT BULB

"It's a comedy. I hope it is. Not a door-slamming comedy and not a bedroom farce. I see it as very much a modest little play, hopefully amusing and engrossing." —Before the premiere of The Floating Light Bulb, The New York Times, *1981*

112. What is the one magic trick that Paul Pollack performs for his father?
  a. He makes his wallet disappear, then reappear from behind his head.
  b. He cuts his mistress in half, then restores her.
  c. He cuts up one of his father's ties, and restores the tie.
  d. He cuts all the hair off his father's head, and then puts it back perfectly in place.

113. Paul performs the floating-light-bulb trick during the play
    a. twice
    b. once
    c. four times
    d. never

"On Broadway, the script is 90 percent of [creativity]. So it's fun to write a play, but a screenplay is not writing, it's not challenging. The movie is made by the director, the actor, and by the editor. So I would have no interest in just screenwriting. . . . I always felt about my first play that once I write the thing, and it opens, they can treat me like a dead author. I don't care if my plays are never made into movies. It wouldn't bother me . . ."
                                                —Cinema, *1972*

7

TAKE THE MONEY
AND RUN

"I don't think anyone else would have made Take the Money and Run *or* Bananas. *I think that for all their flaws and immaturities, you can say that they weren't factory-made films. They were not the usual Hollywood product. I think these films will always be playing around, even fifty years from now, because they represent a certain kind of filmmaking."* —Cinema, *1972*

114. *Take the Money and Run* appears to have been shot all over the country, in dingy anonymous small towns and big cities. In fact, it was all shot in one city. Which one?
   a. New York
   b. Cleveland
   c. San Francisco
   d. Chicago

115. The last scene of the pretitle sequence finds
   a. Virgil, cornered by police shooting at him in an alley, firing his gun—which turns out to be a cigarette lighter
   b. Virgil tossing his cello out the window

    c. Virgil cutting out a pane of glass perfectly from a jew-
       elry store—then stealing the glass instead of the jewelry
    d. Virgil's glasses stepped on by belligerent hoodlums

116. In early documentary footage, Virgil is seen in happier days
with his grandfather. Unfortunately, his grandfather suffers a
serious accident that sends him into permanent delusions that he
is Kaiser Wilhelm. What happens?
    a. He is hit by a crane in midtown Manhattan.
    b. He is punched several times in the groin after trying to
       rob an elderly German woman.
    c. He is struck on the head by a foul ball at Yankee Sta-
       dium.
    d. He is on board the *Lusitania* when it is torpedoed.

*"I used to read a tremendous amount about crime. I knew every-
thing about jail and robberies. I knew the names of all the gang-
sters the way kids list the best all-star teams. I think I would
have made the kind of criminal you see in this film."*
                                  —The New York Times, *1969*

177. Why is Virgil's *first* prison escape foiled?
    a. His fellow inmates forgot to tell him the escape was
       called off.
    b. He mistakes the guard's bathroom for the exit gate.
    c. He tries to tunnel his way out through sand.
    d. His gun, made out of soap, dissolves in the rain.

118. What is the *first thing* Virgil steals in the movie?
    a. a gumball machine
    b. bags of money from a Brinks truck
    c. a gorilla
    d. a woman's purse

119. Virgil's glasses are stepped on a total of seven times during
the course of the movie. At what point does Virgil himself finally
crush his own pair?

Bullies express their opinions
on Virgil's cello playing. *Courtesy
of ABC Video Enterprises*

a. after trying, and failing, to make love to Louise
b. after being sentenced by the judge for his first heist
c. after accidentally disclosing his next bank-robbery plan to two police officers in a coffee shop
d. He never does step on his glasses.

"For the following two weeks I screened a collection of skits that were so original, so charming, so funny in absolutely unexpected ways that it made this period one of the most pleasurable in all my years of editing." —Ralph Rosenblum and Robert Karen, When the Shooting Stops, the Cutting Begins, *1979*

120. Virgil meets Louise (Janet Margolin) in the park, where "after fifteen minutes I wanted to marry her, and after thirty minutes I completely gave up the idea of stealing her purse." In a scene with originally no dialogue, they take a romantic walk in a misty haze. Here Virgil tells us how he knew he was in love, because

a. he was smiling like an idiot
b. he was nauseous
c. he began hyperventilating
d. he began fondling her hat

. . .

FIRST TELLER: That looks like "gub"; that doesn't look like "gun."

SECOND TELLER: Please put fifty thousand dollars into this bag and abt natural . . . What's "abt"?

. . .

121. Until he is arrested after this disastrous bank holdup, Louise thinks Virgil is actually

a. a cellist with the New York Philharmonic
b. executive vice-president of IBM
c. backup guard for the New York Knicks
d. a rocket scientist

"I don't know the first thing about directing . . . so I showed the crew some movies I like in order to explain the abstract feelings I have in a concrete way."   —The New York Times, *1969*

122. Among these films were the then popular *Elvira Madigan* (satirized in Virgil and Louise's loving roll on a deserted beach) and Antonioni's *Blow-Up*. Perhaps the most recognizable takeoff at the time was on *Cool Hand Luke*, in which a loser, convict Paul Newman, squares off against an unsympathetic warden who repeatedly sends him into "The Box." Virgil, too, is sent to solitary. The film's narrator, Jackson Beck, notes, "He complains frequently, and is subject to frequent torture and brutality. For two days, he is _____."
   a. locked in a vat of cement and forced to breathe through a straw
   b. locked in a sweat box with an insurance salesman
   c. locked in a recording studio with Mama Cass
   d. locked in a bathroom with a Greek homosexual

123. Virgil is sent to a maximum-security prison. On the first day at the new prison, he and three inmates are solemnly warned by the warden against trying to escape. The warden asks if there are any questions. What does Virgil ask him?
   a. if it's OK to faint while in the field
   b. if it's OK for a girl to pet on the first date
   c. if it's OK to flirt with a prisoner much bigger than himself
   d. if it's OK for two unmarrieds to make love if they don't share the same religion

124. A prisoner who hasn't given the warden a good day's work is taken into a room for punishment. The warden takes Virgil with him to watch, and Virgil is treated to the sight of
   a. the prisoner tied to a chair and forced to listen to opera
   b. a guard whipping the prisoner with an ear of corn

Janet Margolin.
Courtesy of artist

c. the prisoner whipping the guard, who is enjoying it
d. a guard whipping the prisoner's shadow

125. "The prisoners are served one meal a day," intones the solemn narrator. That meal is
a. a glass of frost
b. a doodle of cheese
c. a plate of yolk
d. a bowl of steam

126. Before planning his second bank robbery, Virgil gathers his gang of bank robbers around him to watch a film on the bank's workings. But first . . . "Ah, there's always a boring short," someone grumbles. An actual short was produced by Jack Rollins and Charles Joffe. Can you name the title?
a. *Whale Hunting in Southern Yemen*
b. *Stalking the Tiger in Mozambique*
c. *Trout Fishing in Quebec*
d. *Taxi Driving in New York City*

127. In the picture at right, Fritz "directs" Virgil's second bank
holdup. In addition to being a once famous movie director who
worked with Valentino and John Gilbert, what else has Fritz
been?

    a. batboy for the New York Yankees
    b. cello soloist for the Vienna Boys Choir
    c. prison commandant at Auschwitz
    d. personal bodyguard to Woodrow Wilson

128. The team of criminals recruited by Virgil for his second bank
robbery is a deadly group, wanted for many offenses. One of the
following, however, does *not* belong. Which one?

    a. wanted for dancing with a mailman
    b. wanted for extortion, burglary, and conspiring to make
       love with the telephone company
    c. wanted for bank robbery, assault with a deadly weapon,
       and getting naked in front of his in-laws
    d. wanted for arson, robbery, and marrying a horse

129. Match the name of the person interviewed with his occupation.

    1. Mr. Torgman   a. probation officer
    2. Mrs. Dorothy Lowry   b. prison shrink
    3. Stanley Krim   c. author of *Mother Was a Red*
    4. T. S. Foster   d. insurance salesman
    5. Daniel Miller   e. cello teacher
    6. Julius Epstein   f. cretin
    7. Joe Green   g. schoolteacher

130. To gain an early parole after his first arrest, Virgil volunteers
to be inoculated with an experimental vaccine. What is the one
side effect?

    a. for eight hours, he becomes a rabbi
    b. for four hours, he becomes a hard-boiled egg
    c. for six hours, he becomes Adolf Hitler
    d. for two hours, he becomes Greta Garbo

"You call zis a bank robbery? I said
action five minutes ago!" *Courtesy of
ABC Video Enterprises*

131. TRUE OR FALSE: Virgil's response to his wife, Louise, when she announces that her Christmas present to him is a forthcoming baby, is "What kind?"

132. After escaping from prison, Virgil keeps a low profile with his first real job, in the mailroom of an insurance company. He is then blackmailed by Miss Blair (Jacqueline Hyde), a co-worker, whom he tries to kill in three different ways. Only *one* of the following is right. Which one?
   a. He tries to stab her with a steak knife.
   b. He sends her a package of dynamite stuffed into Valentine's Day cards.
   c. He tries to suffocate her with a pillow while making love.
   d. He tries to run her over with a car in her living room.

133. When we *first* see Woody as the adult Virgil, he is
   a. being chased by a gorilla after robbing a pet shop
   b. getting his glasses stomped on by an old woman whose purse he tried to snatch
   c. trying to play cello in the marching band
   d. trying to join a street gang

134. During a job interview that soon becomes a "What's My Line?" parody, Virgil, as John Q. Public, discloses his previous occupation after his interviewer fails to guess it. ("Is this something that can be found in the home?") What was the occupation?
   a. manufacturer of escalator shoes for those who get nauseous on escalators
   b. designer of the world's first automatic toothbrush
   c. creator of a pacemaker for prisoners sentenced to the electric chair
   d. maker of shoulder pads for subway commuters

135. In one prison scene, Virgil is assigned to the laundry. In a sight gag edited out of the movie's television version, Virgil is surprised to come across _____ while sifting through the prisoners' laundry.

a. a garter belt
b. a condom
c. a tutu
d. a brassiere

136. Virgil's parents, hilariously played by Ethel Sokolow and Henry Leff, are so ashamed of their worthless progeny that they appear
   a. in silhouette only
   b. disguised in Groucho Marx–like glasses, fake noses, and fake moustaches
   c. clad head to toe in garbage bags
   d. as line drawings

"I was learning, floundering, trying to get by on my sense of humor. When it came to the moment of truth, I felt I could count on the laughs. I depended on the laughs to bail me out."
                                    —The New York Times Magazine, *1979*

8

BANANAS

"For some reason, you get a lot of credit when you touch on politics. But it's not tougher to do. It can be easier to do because there are so many good jokes. I just don't know enough about politics or have much of an interest in it. Bananas *was coincidentally political . . . I really had no point I was trying to make in the whole thing."* —Cinema, *1972*

137. Originally, the title of *Bananas* was to have been
   a. *El Weirdo*
   b. *Coconuts*
   c. *Banana Republic*
   d. *Bonkers*

138. In addition to Howard Cosell, which ABC-TV (at that time) personalities appear in *Bananas*?
   a. Keith Jackson and Bill Beutel
   b. Roger Grimsby and Jim McKay
   c. Don Dunphy and Roger Grimsby
   d. Jim McKay and Bill Beutel

"Woody packed Bananas *so full of jokes that another movie could have been made from its outtakes. If he thought he needed 150 jokes in an hour, he wrote and photographed 300. And he made them tighter, a joke at every turn, so that the pace would never slacken."*   —*Ralph Rosenblum and Robert Karen,* When the Shooting Stops, the Cutting Begins, *1979*

139. During the course of the film, Fielding Mellish tests three products in his job as products tester. Which one did he *not* test?
a. an electrically warmed toilet seat
b. a wind-proof umbrella
c. a coffin wired for stereo
d. an Execusizer

140. Fielding picks up five magazines, four of which are: *Time, Commentary, Saturday Review,* and *Newsweek.* But the man behind the counter only inquires loudly as to the price of the fifth magazine, which is
a. *Orgasm*
b. *Screw*
c. *Copulate*
d. *Teen Beat*

141. Trying to impress the student activist Nancy (Louise Lasser), Fielding notes that on his international travels he went to the Vatican—though not in Rome. "They were doing so well they opened one in _____," says Fielding.
a. Peoria
b. Israel
c. Russia
d. Denmark

142. "I love you, I love you," pants Fielding while making love to Nancy. She asks him to say it in French. He can't but asks if she'll accept it in
a. Arabic
b. Italian

    c. Hebrew

    d. Spanish

143. Upon his arrival in San Marcos, Fielding is ecstatic to be invited to dinner at Colonel Vargas's mansion. Dreamy harp music accompanies him as he repeats "Dinner with the president . . ." Where is it coming from?

    a. a spanish nymphet, hiding under the bed

    b. a young musician practicing in Fielding's closet

    c. the rebel army, marching outside with an orchestra

    d. It doesn't come from anywhere; it just happens to be on the soundtrack.

144. While in the company of the rebels, the villagers, now soldiers, are given instruction on how to suck the poison out of a snakebite. Fielding, however, balks, explaining that he cannot

    a. suck anything out of a person's leg without written permission from a doctor

    b. suck anyone's leg without a note from his mother

    c. suck anyone's leg without going to temple first

    d. suck anyone's leg who he's not engaged to

145. At the president's palace, an orchestra sits on the balcony playing imaginary music, since they have no instruments. (Fielding later requests, "Could you keep it down? . . . I have a headache.") The orchestra has no instruments because

    a. Vargas is afraid that the wrong music could incite revolution

    b. they are not visible to anyone who is not in the government

    c. the music they are playing does not require instruments

    d. the instruments were not delivered to the set on time, and Woody shot the scene without them rather than waste time and money

146. The actor who played Colonel Vargas (see photo) gained fame in the late sixties as the discriminating El Exigente for Savarin coffee. Can you identify him?

Fielding with a present for Colonel Vargas.
Courtesy of United Artists Pictures, Inc.

147. Fielding greatly displeases Colonel Diaz by the time he leaves
the palace. Diaz wants him eliminated at once, mainly because
  a. "he does not even know why his own people cannot eat
     pork"
  b. "he brings cake for a group of people; he doesn't even
     bring an assortment!"
  c. "he has the most expensive dish on the menu; but yet he
     goes half on the check!"
  d. "he brings chocolates for a group of people; he doesn't
     even wrap them"

148. After the rebels seize control, Colonel Diaz is slightly in-
toxicated with his new power. The official language is now Swed-
ish; all boys under sixteen are now sixteen. What new rules apply
to underwear?
  a. It must be changed every two weeks, and must always
     be green.
  b. It must be changed every half hour and worn on the out-
     side.
  c. It must never be changed until San Marcos gets U.S.
     aid.
  d. It must be changed every ten minutes and worn around
     the head.

149. Once he is with the rebels, Fielding marches into a grocery
store and runs up the most spectacular takeout order in history:
1,000 7-Up's, 300 tuna sandwiches, 200 BLT's, 700 coffees, 500
Cokes, and . . . 1,000 grilled cheese sandwiches, 490 of which are
on rye, 300 on white bread, and 110 on whole wheat. Who wants
his on a roll?
  a. Hernandez
  b. Velasquez
  c. Garcia
  d. Fernandez

150. In majestic slow motion, Fielding rips off his clothes, preparing to make love to the rebel woman (played by *Playboy*

centerfold Natividad Abiscal) whom he has charmed. This is or-
chestrated to what musical theme?
   a. the *William Tell* Overture
   b. Beethoven's Fifth
   c. the *1812* Overture
   d. the theme from *Doctor Zhivago*

151. Once Fielding is elected the new leader of San Marcos, he
attends a fund-raiser in New York, in hopes of winning U.S. aid.
After starting off with two abysmal jokes, Fielding nervously
tells the crowd that San Marcos leads the world in
   a. dysentery
   b. cocaine exports
   c. underwear
   d. hernias

152. "The greatest crimes are the crimes against human dignity,"
Fielding notes, and inadvertently proves this
   a. when Nancy tells him he's immature sexually, physically,
      and intellectually
   b. by falling into a manhole
   c. by slamming a locker door on his friend's hand
   d. when his car is towed away

153. In analysis, Fielding notes that his parents beat him from
   a. December 23, 1942, till the late spring of 1944
   b. late winter 1941 till March 8, 1944
   c. New Year's Eve 1942 till Valentine's Day, 1943
   d. summer 1942 till his freshman year of college

*"This trial is a travesty of a mockery of a sham of a mockery
of a travesty of two mockeries of a sham."*
                                        —*Fielding, at his trial*

154. Fielding is eventually arrested by the U.S. government and
brought to stand trial on treason charges. At his trial, the wily
Mellish, acting in his own defense, moves for a mistrial, because

Fielding cross-examines a parrot.
Courtesy of United Artists Pictures, Inc.

    a. there are no homosexuals on the jury
    b. there are no heterosexuals on the jury
    c. the jury is stoned out of its mind
    d. there are no white people on the jury

155. One of the damaging witnesses against Fielding is a large black woman, who actually claims to be _____ in disguise. "I have many enemies," she explains.
    a. Gen. William Westmoreland
    b. Carlo Gambino
    c. J. Edgar Hoover
    d. Bob Dylan

156. After Fielding is found guilty on twelve counts, the judge says he will suspend the fifteen-year sentence if Mellish promises
    a. never to make another movie about politics
    b. never to apply to law school
    c. never to move into the judge's neighborhood
    d. never to make love to an obese woman

157. Howard Cosell "broadcasts" the assassination of the San Marcos leader in the opening scene of the movie. He returns for the final scene as well, this time doing the play-by-play for
    a. the assassination of Fielding by Black Panthers
    b. a boxing match between Fielding and Nancy
    c. dinner at the San Marcos White House
    d. the consummation of Fielding and Nancy's marriage on the night of their wedding

"My first two pictures are full of areas ruined by my inexperience. . . . I don't mean lenses or things like that, I mean the inexperience of not knowing how to schedule a thing properly, how to shoot it right, know when to say, 'Don't break the set up, I want to look at it tomorrow.' When I started filming, all they said to me was, 'You'd better not go overbudget, so just keep moving.' " —Cinema, *1972*

9

PLAY IT AGAIN, SAM

"They [the film producers who bought the rights to Sam] didn't want me in it until Bananas started doing well. I wouldn't want to direct. I'm doing it to get more people in to see my films."
—The New York Times, *1971*

Complete the Quote and Name the Participants

Q1. "My parents never got divorced, though I _____."

Q2. "How can it be a sexual problem? We weren't even _____."

Q3. "I was incredible in bed last night. I never once had to sit up and consult _____."

Q4. "I love the rain. It washes _____ off the _____ of life."

Q5. "I wanna have your _____."

"This is a character study of an extreme neurotic who engages in a million thoughts, pro and con, before taking any action."
—Seventeen, *1972*

158. The Broadway version of *Play It Again, Sam* was set in New York, as the film, directed by Herbert Ross, was supposed to be. Why was it finally shot in San Francisco?

    a. At the last minute, Woody decided San Francisco was a more logical location, because it had the highest suicide record in the U.S.

    b. Diane Keaton was shooting another film there at the time.

    c. New York was hit by a film technicians' strike.

    d. The film was prohibitively expensive to shoot in New York.

159. Why did Allan's wife Nancy (Susan Anspach) wind up leaving him?

    a. She wanted to laugh more.

    b. She wanted to go across Europe on a motorcycle.

    c. He wasn't romantic.

    d. All of the above.

160. TRUE OR FALSE: In the film, as in the play, *Play It Again, Sam* begins and ends with scenes from *Casablanca*.

161. Preparing for a blind date with Sharon (Jennifer Salt), a photographer's assistant, Allan can't decide what music to put on (he will eventually wind up accidentally flinging the record over his shoulder in a nervous moment). The record is by

    a. Bartok

    b. The Beatles

    c. Oscar Peterson

    d. Tony Bennett

162. What does Allan originally want to tell Sharon about his wife?

    a. that she left him for a lesbian

    b. that she took yoga and est and became a fruit fly

    c. that she was killed in a mine accident

    d. that she became a man

Diane Keaton, Woody, and Jerry Lacy as the
"transparent" Bogart in *Play It Again, Sam* on
Broadway, 1966. *Courtesy of Philippe Halsman*

163. "I gotta cut down on my drinking . . . I'm putting away a quart a day," Allan tells Sharon with macho swagger. What does he tell her he drinks?
   a. vodka
   b. tonic water
   c. rye
   d. bourbon

164. At an art gallery, Allan is rejected by a girl he asks out for a Saturday-night date because she's committing suicide. What is his response?
   a. "D'you need a makeup person?"
   b. "What are you doing Sunday?"
   c. "What are you doing Friday night?"
   d. "Can we double?"

"We both have our definite problems. I understand him and he understands me. When I first read for the part in the play, I remember thinking that Woody seemed as scared of me as I was of him." —Diane Keaton, The New York Times, 1971

165. What is the first sign in the film that Allan and Linda (Diane Keaton) have more in common than she does with her husband Dick (Tony Roberts)?
   a. They both suck TV dinners frozen.
   b. They both like to take Darvon with apple juice.
   c. They both threw up in the same United Airlines terminal.
   d. They both drink bourbon and water.

166. After Allan and Linda finally make love, they are virtually dwarfed by a Humphrey Bogart poster dominating the bedroom wall. From which movie?
   a. *The African Queen*
   b. *Across the Pacific*
   c. *Treasure of the Sierra Madre*
   d. *The Barefoot Contessa*

167. After dropping off Linda following a night of passionate lovemaking, Allan is unbearably happy—so happy that, as he walks, he
  a. pushes a man into the Bay
  b. fondles a policewoman
  c. pushes a construction worker into a manhole
  d. jumps off the Golden Gate Bridge

168. Allan has four fantasies of how Dick may react when he finds out about the affair. The first finds an elegantly clad Dick and Allan trading clever quips with Noël Coward–style sophistication. The second finds Dick walking into the ocean to drown himself. In the third, Dick catches a plane to Alaska, asking Allan to take care of Linda. What is the fourth?
  a. Dick, as a Mafia kingpin, gives Allan the kiss of death before a henchman blows him away.
  b. Dick and Bogart team up to steal Linda back.
  c. Dressed as bakers, Dick and Allan fight a duel with knives.
  d. Allan, talking with Bogart toughness, tells a despairing Dick, "Dat's da way it goes, kid."

169. What is Allan's fear of making love on the beach?
  a. He'll fall in quicksand.
  b. He'll score and drown at the same time.
  c. He'll wind up served as an hors d'oeuvre for sharks.
  d. He'll score with a red jellyfish.

170. How many times does the Bogart figure make an appearance?
  a. five times
  b. ten times
  c. seven times
  d. three times

171. When does Allan witness, through his imagination, the death of Bogart?
  a. while making love to Linda
  b. while at the supermarket, buying food for a dinner date with Linda

    c. saying good-bye to Linda at the airport

    d. sitting on the couch with Linda, trying to get up the nerve to make a pass at her

172. "How could I misread those signs?" asks Allan, after

    a. he is rejected sexually by a nymphomaniac

    b. he is rejected sexually by Linda

    c. he is slapped by his blind date

    d. he is kissed by Dick

173. While frantically trying to reach Linda, who keeps hanging up on him, Allan finally gets through. But he's dialed a wrong number. Who has he reached?

    a. a Chinese laundromat

    b. the FBI

    c. a health spa

    d. *Screw* magazine

174. The film ends with Allan left alone at the airport after Linda has flown off to Cleveland with Dick. At the end of the play, however,

    a. Dick gets on the plane by himself, and Linda goes off with Allan

    b. Allan sneaks onto the plane with both of them, and there is a duel over Linda

    c. Allan meets a responsive new girl friend, with the same tastes he has

    d. Allan goes off to the movies, to watch *Casablanca* yet another time

"Just writing *for the screen, I think, is a real dumb job. What's creative is directing and acting on the screen. Whereas on Broadway all the creativity is with the writer. I sold* Don't Drink the Water *to films, and I couldn't care less if they made it into a musical, or made it into a terrible movie, which they did. When I sold* Sam, *I couldn't care less who they got to play it. As it happens, they got me. So I devoted a little interest to it."*

                                      —Cinema, *1972*

10

GETTING EVEN
Fiction Collection No. 1

"I want people to read my stories without the slightest investment of intellect and laugh . . . I don't want them to have to read through two paragraphs of erudite references. I want them to start laughing almost immediately."
—*In Eric Lax*, On Being Funny: Woody Allen and Comedy, *1975*

175. *Getting Even* contains the first story Woody sent to *The New Yorker*, which was bought. ("I thought, Well, I'm never going to sell them anything again in my life," Woody recalls.) As everyone by now knows, the story was the beginning of a wonderful friendship. . . . Which story was it?
   a. "Hassidic Tales"
   b. "Conversations with Helmholtz"
   c. "My Philosophy"
   d. "The Gossage-Vardebedian Papers"

176. "I'm at a dinner party with some friends when suddenly a man walks in with a bowl of soup on a leash." This is the beginning of a dream in "The Metterling Lists," told by Metterling to
   a. Carl Jung
   b. his poodle

c. Franz Kafka
d. Sigmund Freud

177. In "A Look at Organized Crime," Woody parodies the colorful nicknames of Mafia figures, particularly Lucky Luciano. Here it's Lucky Lorenzo, so named when
    a. a bomb that went off in his hat failed to kill him
    b. his wife was forced to pay alimony to *him*
    c. a bullet aimed at his heart went through his pinkie
    d. he filed his income tax late and got a refund

178. The other Mafia figures are the victims of some ingenious deaths. Match the Mafia character with the method by which he was killed:

1. Kid Lipsky	a. The Squillante Construction Company was erected on the bridge of his nose.
2. Dominick Mione	
3. Guiseppe Vitale	
4. Gaetano Santucci	b. Dressed as a mouse at what he thought was a costume party, he was riddled with bullets.
5. Irish Larry Doyle	
6. Vincent Columbraro	
	c. was locked in a closet from which all the air was sucked out through a straw
	d. His head was made into a wind instrument.
	e. He was returned in 27 separate mason jars.
	f. not seen in 46 years since stepping into a hot tub

179. Once initiated into the Mafia, a man is not permitted to eat chutney, to amuse his friends by imitating a hen, or to
    a. kill anybody named Ginsberg
    b. kill anybody named Papaganzwych
    c. kill anybody named Vito
    d. kill anybody

180. In the parody of historical memoirs, "The Schmeed Memoirs," Albert Speer recalls that he didn't know Hitler was a Nazi; for many years he thought he worked for
    a. the National Football League
    b. the phone company
    c. the post office
    d. the Lexington School for the Deaf

· · ·

*F*ill in the following two aphorisms of "My Philosophy."

181. "It is impossible to experience one's own _____ objectively and still carry a _____."
    a. orgasm; bag of groceries
    b. singing; pack of gum
    c. death; tune
    d. nakedness; telephone

182. "Not only is there no _____, but try getting a _____ on weekends."
    a. God; plumber
    b. justice; divorce
    c. reason to live; taxi
    d. heaven; date

183. In Woody's parody of college courses ("Spring Bulletin") one course is rapid reading, in which students will be expected, by the end of the term, to be able to read in fifteen minutes which of the following?
    a. *Ulysses*
    b. *Remembrance of Things Past*
    c. *The Brothers Karamazov*
    d. the Yellow Pages

184. In the first of Woody's "Hassidic Tales," a man journeys to Chelm to seek the advice of Rabbi Ben Kaddish, asking him where he can find peace. What is the rabbi's response?

a. He smashes him in the head with a candlestick after telling the man to turn around.
b. He brings forth two sleek Hong Kong hookers.
c. He directs him to hold his head under the East River for forty minutes.
d. He buries him in ten feet of sand.

185. Rabbi Zwi Chaim Yisroel, an Orthodox rabbi and intellectual, is shocked when a woman asks him why Jews are not allowed to eat pork. ("We're *not*?") In Woody's mock interpretation, scholars believe that the Torah merely suggested
a. not eating pork on Jewish holidays
b. not eating pork with cheese blintzes
c. not eating pork on weekends
d. not eating pork at certain restaurants

186. TRUE OR FALSE: The chess-by-mail competition between Gossage and Vardebedian ("The Gossage-Vardebedian Papers") is won by Gossage.

187. In "A Twenties Memory," Woody recounts a fictional time spent with Ernest Hemingway (sending up Papa's descriptive style). When does Hemingway *first* break his nose?
a. boxing in Africa, after Woody kids him about his new beard
b. deep-sea diving in the Peloponnese, after Woody kids him about bullfighting
c. at Jack Dempsey's training camp, after Woody kids him about his forthcoming novel
d. in Gertrude Stein's boudoir, after Woody kids him about yet another touchy subject

188. During the same time period, Woody meets Scott and Zelda Fitzgerald. By this time, Zelda's disruptive influence has limited Scott's literary output to
a. an occasional work of graffiti and two periods
b. an occasional seafood recipe and a series of commas

   c. an occasional obituary and a group of semicolons
   d. an occasional train schedule and four apostrophes

189. In "Conversations with Helmholtz," the good doctor is best known for his experiments in behavior, in which he proved that
   a. death is an acquired trait
   b. death is hereditary
   c. death is late
   d. death is a bigot

190. What caused the final break in the feuding Helmholtz-Freud relationship?
   a. Helmholtz's preference for halibut
   b. Freud's annoying habit of imitating a yak
   c. Helmholtz's aversion to breathing
   d. Freud's death

191. The use of the fake ink blot ("The Discovery and Use of the Fake Ink Blot") was discovered by
   a. a team of cardiologists dressed up as hens for a Halloween party
   b. a team of biologists in Hong Kong to buy suits
   c. a team of CIA agents stranded for a night in a Soviet brothel
   d. a team of zoologists meeting at a leper colony

192. In "Mr. Big," Woody's tough-talking detective, Kaiser Lupowitz, is hired by a bright young college girl to find
   a. a sex pervert
   b. her diaphragm
   c. Jimmy Hoffa
   d. God

?11

EVERYTHING YOU ALWAYS WANTED TO KNOW ABOUT SEX (BUT WERE AFRAID TO ASK)

"This is a very personal view of sex. I don't think everybody conceives of sex the way I do—surrealistic and rich with humor. I couldn't have made this movie ten years ago, but it's not graphic, clinical, or full of nudity. I'm in no way exploiting the taboo side of sex. The language is sexual, but I've treated it as if I were making a movie about cattle ranching."

—The New York Times, *1972*

193. *Sex* was Woody's first United Artist film shot entirely in a Hollywood studio, under a strict two-million-dollar budget. But Woody was not the original director intended for the adaptation of David Reuben's best-seller. Paramount Pictures optioned the book as a star vehicle for an actor who, at the time (late sixties–early seventies) was considered "perfect" for the subject. Who was he?

- a. Warren Beatty
- b. Elliott Gould
- c. Michael Caine
- d. James Coburn

194. In the first sketch, entitled "Do Aphroaisiacs Work?," the King summons his fool for comic relief, but, as he bellows later,

"He's not funny!" According to one of the Fool's jokes, the King
is the only man who can
    a. hump the Queen while shaving
    b. masturbate while doing push-ups
    c. swim the moat lengthwise
    d. shoot a slingshot with his hairpiece

195. Two scenes from *Hamlet* are invoked in this sketch. They
are
    a. act 1, scene 4; act 3, scene 1
    b. act 2, scene 1; act 5, scene 1
    c. act 3, scene 4; act 3, scene 1
    d. act 1, scene 5; act 4, scene 3

196. The Fool is warned by palace guards that if he is caught
with the Queen, the King will cut off his legs, arms, and head.
What is the Fool's response to this threat?
    a. "Five out of six isn't bad."
    b. "Oh. All my secondary parts."
    c. "As long as I retain a sense of dignity."
    d. "Why stop there?"

197. How does the Fool defend himself when the King catches
him hiding in the Queen's bed?
    a. He claims the Renaissance has just arrived and it's OK
       to sleep around.
    b. He doesn't, but invites the King to share his wife and
       anticipate the twentieth century.
    c. He reveals that *he* is wearing the Queen's chastity belt.
    d. He recalls that the King told him to look up his wife if
       he was ever in town.

198. The picture at right relates to the film's second sketch, "What
Is Sodomy?" What is happening in the scene?
    a. Dr. Ross (Gene Wilder) has taken Daisy, the sheep, to a
       hotel room for an illicit affair, to put it mildly.
    b. Dr. Ross is examining the sheep for scratch marks.

Romancing the sheep. *Courtesy
of United Artists Pictures, Inc.*

    c. Dr. Ross, stunned to find the sheep in his bed, is trying to coax her out the door.

    d. The sheep has just told Dr. Ross she's returning to Argentina.

199. When does Dr. Ross's wife first become suspicious that her husband may be having an affair?

    a. when he begins to baa in bed

    b. when he wakes up at 3:00 A.M. with a craving for lamb chops

    c. when he spends a Saturday morning munching the lawn

    d. when he is caught fondling his lambs-wool sweater

200. What is Dr. Ross doing in the sketch's last shot, after he has been abandoned by his wife and sheep?

    a. drinking from a bottle of Woolite

    b. examining the legs of chickens in a restaurant

    c. applying for work in a pet store

    d. forlornly standing on a deserted field in Argentina

201. In the Italian movie parody sketch ("Why Do Some Women Have Trouble Reaching Orgasm?") Fabrizio notes that, when making love in public, his wife comes like

    a. Mt. St. Helens

    b. an express train

    c. Niagara Falls

    d. a speeding bullet

202. What kind of car does Fabrizio drive?

    a. a gray Lamborghini

    b. a white Porsche

    c. a green Mercedes

    d. a red Ferrari

203. In the game-show sketch, entitled "What's My Perversion?," what is the perversion of the show's first guest, Bernard Joffee?

    a. He likes to molest little children with a Dustbuster.

    b. He likes to watch people make love in cat litter.

    c. He likes to expose himself on subways.

Lou Jacobi.
Courtesy of artist

d. He likes to play with himself on the express line of su-
permarkets.

204. Rabbi Ch'aim Bamel, the winner of the weekly contest for
best perversion, gets to have his realized on the show. He is first
tied up and spanked by a model. What is the final part of the
perversion?
  a. The model performs a strip-tease while reciting the
     Torah.
  b. His wife sits at his feet eating pork.
  c. He is cursed at in Hebrew by a Catholic schoolgirl.
  d. He is baptized by a nymphet nun wearing horns.

205. TRUE OR FALSE: The panelists and host of "What's My
Perversion?" were all real-life game-show regulars playing them-
selves.

206. What is the title of the book written by Victor, in the sketch
entitled "Are the Findings of Doctors Who Do Sexual Research
Accurate?"
  a. *Advanced Sexual Positions, and How to Achieve Them
     Without Laughing*

Among the stars of *Sex* were *from left*: Lynn Redgrave, Gene Wilder, Burt Reynolds, and Tony Randall. *Courtesy of artists*

b. *Coital Interruption and Its Relation to Fascism*
c. *Fifty Sexual Positions for the Married Man*
d. *Oral Sex: How to Enjoy It Free of Guilt*

207. The mad scientist, Dr. Bernardo (John Carradine), has discovered in his ground-breaking research that the average length of a man's penis is
  a. eight inches
  b. three feet
  c. ten inches
  d. nineteen inches

208. Victor and his companion, Susan (Heather MacRae), on a tour of the mad doctor's lab, witness three experiments. Which of the following experiments was shown?
  a. two men having sex with a female chimpanzee
  b. a female police officer making love to the brain of a bank robber

    c. a man making love to an enormous rye bread
    d. a lesbian performing fellatio on a wind instrument

209. Dr. Bernardo was termed "insane" by Masters and Johnson after
    a. he filled a condom with nitrogen
    b. he existed on a daily diet of sperm
    c. he built a four-hundred-foot diaphragm
    d. he built a three-hundred-foot vibrator

210. "I know how to handle tits," Victor says confidently before tackling the giant breast that is terrifying the countryside. How does he subdue it?
    a. He sucks out the milk with a huge straw.
    b. He waves the sign of the cross.
    c. He beats it with a leather whip.
    d. He doesn't subdue it, but enjoys it for all it's worth.

211. In the final sketch, "What Happens During Ejaculation?," what remark from the Girl assures the brain-room controller that intercourse will be completed?

    a. "I studied the Hegelian theory while at the Sorbonne in
       Paris."
    b. "I like Peter Fonda movies."
    c. "I completed my thesis in irrational perspectives of social
       philosophy in the 1950s."
    d. "I'm a graduate of New York University."

212. What are the men in the erection room singing as they pump
it up?
    a. "The Star-Spangled Banner"
    b. "A Hard Day's Night"
    c. "Amazing Grace"
    d. "The Hallelujah Chorus"

213. What is Sperm No. 2's last line as he is launched into the
ovum?
    a. "I hope he's not a homosexual."
    b. "Well . . . at least he's Jewish."
    c. "I better make it . . . suppose she's on the Pill?"
    d. "We're gonna make babies!"

214. In a sketch removed before the American release, entitled
"What Makes a Man Homosexual?," Woody plays a spider who
is devoured by a female black widow (Louise Lasser) after orgasm. The sketch was replaced (by "What Are Sex Perverts?")
because
    a. entomologists all over the country threatened to sue
       United Artists
    b. homosexuals all over the country threatened to sue
       United Artists
    c. Woody never found a suitable ending for the sketch
    d. United Artists was forced to drop it or face an X rating

"There are a lot of people who are going to think Everything
You Always Wanted to Know About Sex . . . *is a dirty movie,
and it's those people I'm counting on."*   —Playboy, *1972*

12

SLEEPER

"Sleeper didn't read funny. I hoped that when I got out there in front of the camera with a big banana peel or in a robot suit I could make it funny, but I didn't know." —Seventeen, *1975*

Complete the Quote and Name the Participants

Q1. "My _____ is my second favorite organ!"

Q2. "Being dead for two hundred years is like _____."

Q3. "_____ and _____ . . . two things that come once in a lifetime."

Q4. "I'm not the heroic type. I was beaten up by _____."

Q5. "Sex is different today. Everybody's _____."

"I've tried to make a marriage here of good verbal gags and a decent relationship with the girl and a nice novel setting and plenty of jokes. It will be interesting to see when we edit it if the relationship will take over or if it will be basically a slapstick film or if all of it will work."

—*As told to Eric Lax, before filming* Sleeper

215. Before Miles Monroe was frozen in 1973, what was his occupation?
   a. vice-president of a sperm bank
   b. part owner of the Happy Carrot Health Food Store
   c. lead singer for the Laguna Men's Glee Club for Gentiles
   d. manager of the New York Pornographic Chess Club

216. How was Earth eventually destroyed while Miles lay frozen
for two hundred years?
   a. Every nuclear power plant in the world blew up simulta-
      neously.
   b. Poland staged an antinuke demonstration.
   c. Richard Nixon got overzealous in his bombing of Hanoi.
   d. Albert Shanker got hold of a nuclear bomb.

217. After he is unfrozen, Miles is questioned on various aspects
of the twentieth century, as well as about famous people. According to Miles, who "donated his ego to Harvard Medical School?"
   a. Norman Mailer
   b. Howard Cosell
   c. Charles De Gaulle
   d. Billy Graham

218. TRUE OR FALSE: Miles Monroe was unfrozen by scientists
because the new country, the Central Parallel of the Americas,
wants him as an example of the failures of twentieth-century
man.

219. What was Miles's only serious political stance while living
in the States?
   a. He once lost at checkers for two weeks in a row.
   b. He once refused to have sex for two hours.
   c. He once boycotted adult bookstores for one month.
   d. He once refused to eat grapes for twenty-four hours.

220. "You poor thing," says Luna (Diane Keaton) to Miles, "you
haven't had sex for 200 years!" He corrects her:
   a. "206 if you count leap years."
   b. "210 if you mean sex with another person."

Miles Monroe senses imminent danger.
Courtesy of United Artists Pictures, Inc.

    c. "198. I dreamt a lot."
    d. "204 if you count my marriage."

221. At one point, Miles finds a copy of a *New York Times* from the year 1990, in which the lead story is
    a. the CIA's role in spreading venereal disease
    b. Billy Graham's addiction to heroin
    c. the pope's wife giving birth to twins
    d. Richard Nixon being arrested for molesting a goat

222. According to Luna, all men are presently impotent, except for those whose ancestors were
    a. Irish
    b. Jewish
    c. Italian
    d. Polish

"I was thinking about Sleeper *in terms of how I hate machines in real life. I have no patience with them. I break them. People close to me will confirm how many toasters I've broken."*
           —*As told to Eric Lax, during the making of* Sleeper

223. Disguised as a robot, Miles Monroe must serve the guests at Luna's party. He enters her futuristic kitchen, and has a panicky encounter with
    a. a toaster, which begins spewing sparks the moment
       Miles tries to put some rolls inside
    b. a carving board, which suddenly goes berserk and begins
       chasing Miles with his own knife
    c. instant pudding, which transforms itself into a giant blob
       that must be beaten into submission with a broom
    d. Jell-O, which immediately wraps itself around Miles,
       threatening to suffocate him

224. Miles did find one machine that was in perfect working order, even after two hundred years. What was it?

  a. a Volkswagen
  b. an IBM Selectric
  c. a Sony clock radio
  d. a Swiss grandfather clock

225. In homage to Harold Lloyd, Miles is seen hanging precariously outside the walls of a building, supported only by
  a. bedsheets
  b. bubble gum
  c. piano wire
  d. computer tape

226. What are the names of the two Jewish tailor robots who run the computerized fitting service?
  a. Ginsberg and Epstein
  b. Cohen and Greenberg
  c. Rabinowitz and Greenthal
  d. Ginsberg and Cohen

227. The underground tries to reprogram Miles from the government's brainwashing, reenacting a Flatbush dinner scene in which Miles comes home to tell his parents about his divorce. But their treatment backfires when Miles suddenly becomes
  a. King Lear
  b. Blanche DuBois
  c. Willy Loman
  d. Lassie

228. At a government brainwashing session, Miles, electronically projected into his past, winds up winning the Miss America contest. Which candidate is he?
  a. Miss Montana
  b. Miss Alabama
  c. Miss New York
  d. Miss Hawaii

229. Who was "a Trotskyite who became a Jesus freak and was arrested for selling pornographic connect-the-dots books"?

a. Harold, Luna's boyfriend
b. Erno
c. Lisa Sorenson, an old girl friend of Miles's
d. Dr. Orva

230. "Lots of little guys in tweed suits cutting up frogs on foundation grants." What is Miles describing?
a. biology class
b. organic chemistry
c. science
d. his friends at the orphanage

231. "I'm not up to a performance . . . I'll rehearse with you, if you like." What is Miles referring to when he tells Luna this?
a. *A Streetcar Named Desire*
b. *Madama Butterfly*
c. dinner with her parents
d. sexual relations

232. TRUE OR FALSE: The inspiration for the character's last name came from Woody's admiration of basketball star Earl Monroe.

13

LOVE AND DEATH

*"**A** comedy about death and one's existence in a godless universe . . . the commercial possibilities were immediately apparent to me. Sight gags and slapstick sequences about despair and emptiness. Dialogue jokes about anguish and dread. Finality, mortality, human suffering, anxiety. In short, the standard ploys of the professional funnyman."* —Esquire, *1975*

Complete the Quote and Name the Participants

Q1. "The worst thing you can say about Him is that basically He's an _____."

Q2. "I'll bring the tea bags. We could run a quick check on your _____."

Q3. "Honey, I've been in the mood since _____."

Q4. "Socrates is a man. All men are mortal. All men are Socrates. That means all men are _____."

Q5. "Everyone is obsessed with sex, except for some men who don't think about sex at all. They become _____."

233. Who is killed putting up a lightning rod during an electrical storm?

Boris Grushenko's flashy
onscreen entrance. *Courtesy of
United Artists Pictures, Inc.*

    a. Father Nicolai
    b. Old Gregory
    c. Old Nehamkin
    d. Ivan Grushenko

234. What is Boris's response to his cousin Sonia's (Diane Keaton's) assertion that she is "half saint, half whore"?
    a. "Here's hoping I get the half that sleeps."
    b. "Here's hoping I get the half that eats."
    c. "Here's hoping I get the half that procreates."
    d. "Here's hoping I get the half that beats."

235. Why does Boris think Napoleon (James Tolkan) has invaded Russia?
    a. He thinks Napoleon has run out of Courvoisier.
    b. He thinks Napoleon hasn't gotten laid in a while.
    c. He thinks Napoleon is trying for Best Supporting Actor in the film.
    d. He thinks Napoleon wants to open a croissant shop in Leningrad.

236. "I hear their women don't believe in sex after marriage," Boris tells fellow soldiers as they walk in the forest. He is referring to
    a. Russians
    b. Catholics
    c. Jews
    d. Buddhists

237. When we first see Napoleon, what is he raging over?
    a. the heels on his boots, which still leave him very short
    b. the fear that a cake to be named after him will not be completed before beef Wellington
    c. the fact that everyone is trying to walk like him
    d. the fact that he's losing Anna Karenina to Count Vronsky

238. After being spurned by Boris's brother Ivan ("I should've told you sooner," he grunts, having proposed to someone else),

Sonia, not to be outdone, proposes, on the spot, to the elderly Minskov. He is so happy that he
    a. breaks into a kazatsky and tears three muscles
    b. falls asleep
    c. jumps her, in front of a horrified group of relatives
    d. promptly drops dead

239. How is Ivan eventually killed in the war?
    a. He is shot out of a cannon into a pitchfork.
    b. He accidentally swallows a stick of dynamite.
    c. He dies in childbirth.
    d. He is bayoneted by a Polish conscientious objector.

240. Why is Boris unconcerned when his comrades, furious because he is afraid to fight, ask him what he'll do when the French rape his sister?
    a. He knows his sister will enjoy it.
    b. His sister is fighting in the French underground.
    c. He doesn't have a sister.
    d. His sister looks like Bela Lugosi.

241. At the beginning of the battle, Boris is seen not as a soldier but as
    a. a cheerleader
    b. a blini vendor
    c. a babushka
    d. the master of ceremonies

242. After losing a duel over her honor, Voskovec, the herring merchant that Sonia wound up marrying, lies dying in bed, while Sonia tries to act as if she cares. Sonia notes that she could have been a better wife, conceding that
    a. "I could've slept next to you in bed without my overcoat."
    b. "I suppose I could've gone with you on our honeymoon."
    c. "I know this is the only time you've seen me since we were married."
    d. "I could've made love to you more often . . . or once, even."

243. Why does Sonia finally agree to marry Boris, on the eve of his duel with Count Anton?
   a. She thinks he's going to be killed.
   b. She's already flipped a coin to decide.
   c. She finds him incredibly sexy because he's fighting a duel.
   d. She wants to sublimate his sexual tensions.

244. Distraught over Boris's wishes to commit suicide, Sonia calls on a wrinkled, bearded sage—"the most wrinkled man in the country"—for advice. Lately, though, he seems to have found a general solution for everything. What is it?
   a. blond twelve-year-old girls, two whenever possible
   b. sesame noodles
   c. three black lesbians
   d. all of the above

245. In bed on their wedding night, Boris finally makes his long-anticipated advance toward Sonia. What is her response?
   a. "It's about time."
   b. "We just ate."
   c. "Why?"
   d. "Not here."

*"**I** guess I equate dread with romance, which is why I'm not invited to more parties. The trick, as I see it, is to be Bryonic without appearing moronic. Malraux spoke to me about art being the last defense against death. That, to me, is romantic."*
                              —*As told to Eric Lax,* On Being Funny:
                                 Woody Allen and Comedy, *1975*

246. After Ivan's death, his widow and Sonia divide up his possessions. What does Sonia receive?
   a. his moustache, some string, and all his letters
   b. his moustache, some string, and the vowels from his letters

   c. his moustache, some string, and the consonants from his
      letters
   d. his moustache, some string, and the white lines of his
      letters

247. What is Boris's response, after the first day of battle, when he comes upon the field covered with the corpses of his Russian comrades, only fourteen of whom remain alive?
   a. "That army cooking will get you every time."
   b. "Lucky this is only the exhibition season."
   c. "Looks like we won."
   d. "It's lucky God is on our side."

248. In the picture at right, Sonia, who's been letting Napoleon come on to her, urges Boris to assassinate the great leader. What is Napoleon's initial exclamation?
   a. "Don't shoot—my éclair isn't finished yet."
   b. "You are pointing the wrong side at me."
   c. "Put down your gun—she's over eighteen."
   d. "Go ahead—make my day."

249. "I never want to get married. I just want to get divorced." Who says this?
   a. Don Francisco's wife
   b. Sonia's cousin, Natasha
   c. Boris's mother
   d. Napoleon

250. After Boris is executed, he comes back, with Death, to say his final good-byes to Sonia and Natasha, who are not exactly distraught ("I'm dead; they're talking about wheat," Boris sighs). Sonia asks Boris how it feels to be dead. He tells her it's worse than
   a. spending an evening at the Ice Capades
   b. his Uncle Sasha's acne
   c. shaking hands in a leper colony
   d. the chicken at Tresky's restaurant

Courtesy of United Artists
Pictures, Inc.

251. The "Russian" setting of *Love and Death* is actually
  a. Hungary and Czechoslovakia
  b. Finland and France
  c. France and Hungary
  d. Austria and England

"I'm getting more intellectual, more aggressive. In Love and Death, *I keep spouting jokes, I'm outspoken and brash and undisguisedly interested in intellectual subjects. I used to have confidence in myself mainly as a writer, very little as a performer. Now I'm taking the burden of getting laughs on myself, rather than writing a script that looks funny when you read it."*
                                          —Seventeen, *1975*

?14

WITHOUT FEATHERS
Fiction Collection No. 2

"It's an unprententious book . . . the subject matter is the same as my movie scripts. I'll continue to write a certain number of them for The New Yorker, *but I'm better off trying to put comic prose into a novel."* —Seventeen, *1975*

252. In "Selections from the Allen Notebooks," the narrator twice attempts suicide, the first time by wetting his nose and inserting it into a light socket, and the second by

    a. inhaling next to an insurance salesman
    b. inhaling next to a vat of cat litter
    c. inhaling next to a hare krishna
    d. strangling himself with a loaf of Wonder Bread

253. In the same musings, who is it that tells the narrator: "To block hats—that is everything"?

    a. his sister
    b. his mother
    c. his father
    d. his tailor

254. It was Kruger, Freud's disciple, who discovered sexuality
   a. in chives
   b. in Hershey bars
   c. in French toast
   d. in bacon

255. Match the characters in "Examining Psychic Phenomena" with their experiences:

1. J. C. Dubbs	a. sang "I Got Rhythm" in mourning a nephew's death
2. Albert Sykes	
3. Fenton Allentuck	b. saw the ghost of his dead brother flicking chickens at his bed
4. J. Martinez	
5. Sybil Seretsky's goldfish	c. could make his father's false teeth jump out of his mouth just by concentrating
6. Archilles Londos	
	d. in a precognitive dream, saw his grandfather run over after waltzing with a clothing dummy
	e. spirit left his body to call the Moscowitz Fiber Company
	f. awoke to find his bed had floated to sea, after dreaming he won the Irish Sweepstakes

. . .

Complete the following two Laws and Proverbs from "The Scrolls."

256. The lion and the calf may lie down together but
   a. the calf will not get past second base
   b. the calf will sleep on the floor
   c. the calf won't get much sleep
   d. the calf won't need a night light

257. My Lord, My Lord,
   a. where the hell art Thou?
   b. what hast Thou done lately?
   c. what hast Thou wreaked on my sex life?
   d. what dost Thou take me for?

258. In "The Whore of Mensa," the "whores" are actually
   a. laundresses who will clean anything for a price
   b. gluttons who will finish anyone's dinner for a price
   c. intellectuals who will discuss any subject for a price
   d. neurotics who will dispense guilt for any price

259. According to Woody's philosophy about youth and age ("The Early Essays"), the true test of a man's maturity is how he reacts to
   a. awakening in the Midtown area wearing only his shorts
   b. a blind date who arrives at his house dressed like a squid
   c. finding his bathrobe pockets filled with shaving cream
   d. watching an educational film on human anatomy

260. In "A Brief, Yet Helpful, Guide to Civil Disobedience," Woody notes that the oppressors never revolt and attempt to become the oppressed because it would entail
   a. changing Social Security numbers
   b. a change of underwear
   c. changing the dinner menu
   d. changing locks on the doors

261. The Russian Revolution finally erupted when
   a. the serfs got tired of eating herring
   b. the serfs realized the czar and the tsar were the same person
   c. the serfs realized that no one under six feet could own land
   d. the serfs realized it was 1919 and the revolution hadn't started yet

262. One of the following is *not* a recommended miscellaneous method of civil disobedience:

a. dressing like a policeman and skipping
b. pretending to be an artichoke but punching people as
   they pass
c. standing in front of city hall dressed as a Cornish hen
d. phoning members of the "establishment" and singing
   "Bess You Is My Woman" into the phone

263. What story in *Without Feathers* was published on the op-ed
page of the *New York Times*?
   a. "No Kaddish for Weinstein"
   b. "A Brief, Yet Helpful, Guide to Civil Disobedience"
   c. "But Soft . . . Real Soft"
   d. "If the Impressionists Had Been Dentists"

264. Match the "fabulous tale" with the "mythical beast" from
the story of the same name:

1. The Nurk	a. sea monster with the body of a
2. Flying Snoll	crab and the head of a CPA
3. The Frean	b. reputed to sleep for a thousand
4. The Great Roe	years and suddenly rise in flames
5. The Weal	c. bird two inches long that refers to
	itself in the third person
	d. a lizard with 400 eyes: 200 for dis-
	tance, 200 for reading
	e. large mouse with the lyrics to the
	song "Am I Blue?" printed on its
	stomach

265. Who is the letter-writing artist of "If the Impressionists
Had Been Dentists"?
   a. van Gogh
   b. Degas
   c. Cézanne
   d. Monet

266. In "No Kaddish for Weinstein," Weinstein is puzzled to be
paying four hundred dollars a week for child support to his ex-
wife Harriet, since

   a. the children are already married
   b. Weinstein and his wife are still married
   c. they never had kids
   d. Harriet is only pregnant

267. TRUE OR FALSE: According to "Slang Origins," the phrase *take it on the lam* derives from an English game called "lamming," played with dice and a large tube of ointment.

"I think that when you're writing literary things the fun has to be in the writing of them because there's very little feedback on them. I'm never around when anyone reads them after all. . . ."
—Saturday Review, *1980*

15

THE FRONT

*"**I** have no yen to be a dramatic actor. I didn't look at* The Front *as my chance to play Hamlet. I didn't prepare [for the role] in any special way. I wouldn't know where to begin to prepare."*
—The New York Times, *1976*

268. "I decided to take a chance. From the beginning, I had enormous reservations about doing a film which I had not written and over which I had no directorial control." Woody said this before the opening of *The Front*. With all his hesitation, why did he take the chance?

    a. He wanted to have the opportunity to work with Zero Mostel.
    b. He thought the subject matter was worthwhile.
    c. He needed the money.
    d. He secretly thought that perhaps he might wind up directing the movie, or at least his own scenes.

269. Before becoming a front for blacklisted writers, Howard Prince is

a. manager of a dry-cleaning store
b. an assistant in his brother's dress factory
c. cashier at a restaurant
d. a struggling pornography writer

270. TRUE OR FALSE: Director Martin Ritt, screenwriter Walter Bernstein, Zero Mostel (who plays Hecky Brown), and Herschel Bernardi (producer Phil Sussman) were *The Front*'s only real-life blacklist victims from the 1950s.

271. After successfully fronting for his friend Al Miller (Michael Murphy), Howard is summoned to the set of the show. There he meets the lovely script editor, Florence Barrett (Andrea Marcovicci), who notes Howard's "skill" in making his characters people. He modestly replies
a. "If you're gonna write about people, you might as well make them human beings."
b. "People are some of my favorite persons to be around."
c. "I'm good with people. It's characters I can't write about."
d. "If you're going to write about human beings, you might as well make them people."

272. What did Hecky Brown do six years earlier that first made him a Communist sympathizer?
a. He marched in a May Day parade and signed some "pinko" petitions.
b. He bought a subscription to *Pravda*.
c. He slept with a Russian actress.
d. He had a postwar correspondence with Stalin.

273. Over dinner, Florence tells Howard the biggest sin in her family was to "raise your voice." Howard tells her the biggest sin in *his* family was
a. to buy wholesale
b. to feel guilty
c. to buy retail
d. to have sex after marriage

274. "I've never seen an account like yours . . ." says Howard's bank teller. "Up and down, up and down . . . what do you do?" What does Howard tell him?
   a. He works for the Teamsters.
   b. He manages Elvis Presley.
   c. He works in futures.
   d. He runs the lottery drawing.

275. In the picture at right, Howard finds himself in a pickle: the producers have sent him into an office on the set to do an emergency rewrite on a scene the networks are censoring. What scene is it?
   a. an explicit lesbian tryst in a prison camp
   b. a murder involving an adulterous priest
   c. a scene of a slave auction
   d. a flashback to a concentration camp

276. Accompanying Hecky up to the Catskills, Howard is rejected by a woman on the make when she learns he's a writer. The next time a woman asks him what he does for a living, he's wiser. He claims to be a
   a. dentist
   b. lawyer
   c. shipping mogul
   d. petite model

277. How is Howard's connections to the writers he's working for eventually revealed?
   a. Howard is caught calling one of them after being asked to do another rewrite.
   b. He pours it out to Florence after she tells him she's quit the network.
   c. He is squealed on by Hecky Brown, who looks through Howard's phone book while staying at his house.
   d. Al Miller, tired of Howard getting all the credit, stops giving Howard his scripts, forcing him to fess up.

Tense moments for Howard Prince.
Courtesy of Columbia Pictures

Michael Murphy as Al Miller, the
writer Howard fronts for. *Courtesy of
Columbia Pictures*

Howard tries to convince Florence
Barrett that not being a writer isn't so bad.
Courtesy of Columbia Pictures

278. TRUE OR FALSE. Howard's decisive parting shot to the House Un-American Activities Committee—"Fellas, you can all go fuck yourselves"—is the *only* time a Woody Allen character has uttered an onscreen obscenity.

"In truth, no responsible person in the movie industry ever offered me a serious role before, though occasionally somebody will send me a preposterous script, either a crazy surreal thing about spiders taking over the world, or a dirty story about a sex clinic."
—The New York Times, *1976*

16

ANNIE HALL

"Woody wanted to take a risk and do something different. The first draft was a story of a guy who lived in New York and was forty years old and was examining his life. His life consisted of several strands. One was a relationship with a young woman, another was a concern with the banality of the life that we all live, and a third an obsession with proving himself and testing himself to find out what kind of character he had."
—Co-screenwriter Marshall Brickman on the making of
Annie Hall, *from Ralph Rosenblum and Robert Karen,*
When the Shooting Stops, The Cutting Begins, *1979*

Complete the Quote and Name the Participants

Q1. "Sex with you is really a _____ experience."

Q2. "My grammy never gave gifts, you know? She was too busy getting _____."

Q3. "What'd you do, grow up in a _____ painting?"

Q4. "You are what Grammy Hall would call _____."

Q5. "Those who can't do, teach. Those who can't teach, _____."

"There was a lot of material taken out of that picture that I thought was wonderfully funny . . . I was sorry to lose just about all of that surrealistic stuff. It was originally a picture about me, exclusively, not about a relationship. But sometimes it's hard to foresee at the outset what's going to be the most interesting drift." —Ralph Rosenblum and Robert Karen, When the Shooting Stops, the Cutting Begins, *1979*

279. What was the original title of the movie?
  a. *Annie & Alvy*
  b. *Anhedonia*
  c. *Angst*
  d. *It Had to Be Jew*

"I know it sounds horrible but winning that Oscar for Annie Hall *didn't mean anything to me . . . I have no regard for that kind of ceremony. It has nothing to do with artistic merit. When it's your turn, you win it. . . ."* —Time Out, *1979*

280. TRUE OR FALSE: Woody Allen won an Academy Award for Best Actor for the part of Alvy Singer.

281. *Annie Hall* was not originally intended to be a "nervous romance." In fact, it began not as a film, but as a
  a. science-fiction short story
  b. murder-mystery novel
  c. slapstick farce play
  d. nervous poem

282. As a child, the young Alvy is taken to a doctor, to clear up a depression that is preventing him from doing his homework. What is bothering him?

    a. The number of girls in the world is decreasing.

    b. The universe is expanding.

    c. He has been bullied by the Angel of Death.

    d. He lies in fear of the Coney Island roller coaster destroying his room.

283. At the beginning of the movie, Alvy is waiting for Annie (Diane Keaton) to show up at the Beekman Theater when he is accosted by a beefy fan, who recognizes him from a talk show. Alvy makes a fervent wish to the heavens. What is it?

    a. "I need a large sock of horse manure."

    b. "I need a hot poker iron."

    c. "I need a large polo mallet."

    d. none of the above

284. How does Alvy first meet Annie?

    a. playing tennis with his friend Rob (Tony Roberts), Rob's date, and Annie

    b. standing in front of the Thalia, waiting to see *The Sorrow and the Pity*

    c. at Elaine's, jostling for a corner table

    d. at a yoga class at the Ninety-second Street YMCA

285. "You know the ethics those guys have. It's like a notch underneath child molester." What group is Alvy referring to when he tells this to his first wife?

    a. lawyers

    b. TV producers

    c. gynecologists

    d. politicians

286. After a turbulent lovemaking bout with a *Rolling Stone* reporter, Alvy notes, "Too much emphasis is placed on the orgasm in life." To whom does he attribute the remark?

    a. the Marx Brothers

Alvy Singer and Annie
Hall try to make a good
impression. *Courtesy of
Brian Hamill/Photore-
porters*

   b. Leopold and Loeb
   c. Shirley MacLaine
   d. Nietzsche

287. *Annie Hall* contains one animated sequence, in which the
characters are transported into a fairy tale. Which one?
   a. "Cinderella"
   b. "Sleeping Beauty"
   c. "The Jetsons"
   d. "Snow White and the Seven Dwarfs"

288. In a flashback to an appearance on the Dick Cavett show,
Alvy mentions that he didn't fight in Vietnam because he was
classified 4-H:
   a. "In the event of war, I'm a hostage."
   b. "In the event of war, I'm harmed immediately."

    c. "In the event of war, I'm a homosexual."
    d. "In the event of war, I hyperventilate."

289. *Annie Hall* was filled with a number of cameos from talented New York actors and actresses. Match the actor's name with the role he or she played in the film:

1. Christopher Walken	a. party guest
2. Carol Kane	b. Alvy's date outside the
3. Colleen Dewhurst	Thalia
4. Sigourney Weaver	c. *Rolling Stone* reporter
5. Shelley Duvall	d. Alvy's first wife
6. Jeff Goldblum	e. street stranger
7. Shelley Hack	f. Duane Hall
	g. Mom Hall

290. In the photo at left, Alvy and Annie chat on her terrace about photography, only to be upstaged by subtitles that indicate what each character is *really* thinking. Alvy's first thought is, What a great girl. What is his second thought?
    a. I wonder what she looks like naked.
    b. I wonder if she plays the cello.
    c. This girl is what I would call a real *goy*.
    d. I wonder if she's going to throw up on me like the last one.

291. On their first real date, Alvy stops Annie in the street to get the good-night kiss over with, claiming it will
    a. lead directly to sexual relations
    b. demonstrate his knowledge of French
    c. make him stop drooling
    d. make digestion easier

292. After Easter dinner at the Hall house, Annie's brother, Duane, is driving them to the airport. Inside the car, Alvy is tense because

Featured in *Annie Hall*: Colleen Dewhurst (*top*), Carol Kane (*middle*), Paul Simon (*bottom*), *Courtesy of artists*. Paul Simon: *Courtesy of Warner Brothers Records*

a. Annie has just informed him Duane is a Nazi
b. Duane had earlier expressed a vision of driving head-on into an oncoming car
c. Duane had earlier told Alvy he committed incest with Annie
d. Alvy is having a gastrointestinal attack from Grammy Hall's ham

293. At his beach house in the Hamptons, Alvy is skeptical about the wonderful effects of marijuana, claiming it only offers
a. the illusion that Mick Jagger can sing like Frank Sinatra
b. the illusion that a white man can disco dance
c. the illusion that a white woman will be more like Billie Holiday
d. the illusion that a black man will eat pastrami

294. Twice, Alvy drags Annie to see *The Sorrow and the Pity*, the first time because Annie arrives two minutes too late to see another movie. Which one?
a. Fellini's *La Dolce Vita*
b. Bergman's *Autumn Sonata*
c. Fellini's *8½*
d. Bergman's *Face to Face*

295. What happened to Rob when he played Shakespeare in Central Park?
a. He was beaten over the head with live chickens.
b. Two guys in leather jackets stole his leotards.
c. The actress playing Lady Macbeth tried to kill him.
d. Three guys in war paint mugged him onstage.

"Why go to a city where the only cultural advantage is that I can make a right turn on a red light?"
—Alvy Singer, resisting Rob's suggestion of going to Los Angeles

. . .

Woody satirized a good portion of contemporary culture in *Annie Hall*, none perhaps as mercilessly as Los Angeles. Wheat-germ killers, laugh tracks, and satanic cults were only a few of the city's disadvantages.

. . .

296. What is Alvy's explanation of why there is no garbage in Los Angeles?
  a. "They make it into television shows."
  b. "Like the people, it's not allowed to be seen on the streets."
  c. "It's indistinguishable from the Tudor architecture."
  d. "The Manson Family collects it."

297. At a lavish Christmas party at the house of Tony Lacey (Paul Simon), Woody captures the superficial show-biz ambience with a montage of overheard one-liners. One of these, however, was *not* said:
  a. "I forgot my mantra."
  b. "All the good meetings are taken."
  c. "My Jacuzzi ruptured."
  d. "He really gives good meeting."

298. What does Alvy order on his visit to an L.A. health-food restaurant?
  a. guacamole burger with pita bread
  b. mashed yeast and alfalfa sprouts
  c. cauliflower salad and carrot juice
  d. He brings his own hot dog and french fries.

"Very little of the film is autobiographical . . . I was not born underneath a roller coaster on Coney Island, nor was my first wife politically active, nor was my second wife a member of the literary set, nor did Diane leave me for a rock star to live in California." —From Myles Palmer, Woody Allen: An Illustrated Biography, *1980*

299. TRUE OR FALSE: Diane Keaton's real name is Diane Hall.

300. One incident in the film, according to Woody, *is* based on real life. Which one?
    a. Annie and Alvy trying to catch lobsters
    b. Annie calling Alvy up at 3:00 A.M. to kill a spider
    c. Annie dreaming that she's being strangled by a bespectacled Frank Sinatra
    d. Alvy's dinner at the Hall family house

"There's one clear autobiographical fact in the picture. I've thought about sex since my first intimation of consciousness."
—The New York Times, *1977*

$$ \text{} $$

INTERIORS

"It deals with the spiritual turmoil, the floating unrest that can only be traceable to bad choices in life. Also the apotheosis of the artist beyond his real worth. And how a lover can possess the loved one as an object he can control." —Newsweek, *1978*

301. Where does Arthur (E. G. Marshall) first announce his plans to separate from Eve (Geraldine Page), his wife?
  a. at the beach
  b. in bed
  c. in a furniture store
  d. at dinner

302. Eve is fairly rattled by the announcement. She tells her daughter Joey (Marybeth Hurt) not to
  a. yawn so loudly
  b. breathe so hard
  c. smile like an idiot
  d. cry so much

303. Who describes who as someone "of form without any content"?

Arthur plants an uneasy kiss on Eve's forehead.
Courtesy of United Artists Pictures, Inc.

a. Renata, of Joey
b. Eve, of Arthur
c. Mike, of Renata
d. Frederick, of Flynn

304. After Arthur leaves her for good, what is the first thing Eve is seen doing?
   a. straightening the pillows on the couch
   b. taping the window borders with black tape
   c. taping her eyes shut with white bandages
   d. sitting in church with a gun to her head

305. Arthur marries his new wife, Pearl (Maureen Stapleton), after knowing her for
   a. four weeks
   b. six months
   c. four days
   d. nine months

306. When does Joey blow up at Pearl during the wedding?
   a. when Pearl does the tango with Arthur
   b. when Pearl breaks a vase
   c. when Pearl talks of their trip to Aegina
   d. when Pearl tries to imitate Eve

"At one point, we were changing the furniture in Eve's apartment every half hour and I was getting depressed. Woody pulled me aside and said, 'Don't think it doesn't look great. It does. But I'm not doing comedy now and I'm not sure which direction I'm going now. You'll have to bear with me."
   —*Production Designer Mel Bourne*, The New York Times, *1978*

307. Location scouting for *Interiors* was extensive, as each set had to reflect the sparse and exquisite perfection of the ultimate perfectionist mother, Eve. Fortunately for the crew, the beach scenes were shot at a summer house whose occupants were away. Where were they filmed?

Woody's Three Sisters, before *Hannah*.
Courtesy of United Artists Pictures, Inc.

  a. Quogue
  b. Westhampton
  c. Southhampton
  d. Sag Harbor

308. TRUE OR FALSE: *Interiors* was the last film edited by Woody Allen's longtime editor, Ralph Rosenblum.

309. How does Frederick (Richard Jordan) explain his desire for Flynn (Kristen Griffith), as he tries to rip her clothes off when they are parked outside the house?
  a. He's always regretted marrying Renata (Diane Keaton), not her.
  b. He's tired of making love to a woman with no passion.
  c. He's tired of making love to someone he feels inferior to.
  d. He has suppressed his rage at the whole family for too long.

310. As controversial as the film proved to be with critics, *Interiors* nevertheless received five Oscar nominations. Can you name the correct group of categories?
  a. Best Actress, Best Supporting Actress, Best Art Direction, Best Director, Best Original Screenplay
  b. Best Picture, Best Actor, Best Supporting Actor, Best Editing, Best Cinematography
  c. Best Supporting Actress, Best Original Screenplay, Best Sound Effects, Best Art Direction, Best Editing
  d. Best Actress, Best Director, Best Cinematography, Best Art Direction, Best Screenplay Adapted from Another Medium

"I wanted to make a serious drama about human relationships with no jokes at all, no comedy. I picked the hardest sort of movie to do . . . I think it was very important that I make it, that I face that kind of creative challenge. Still, I have to agree with the critics that the movie was a failure. . . . If I made the film again now, I'd do a lot of things differently and I feel it would be a better movie." —Saturday Review, *1980*

MANHATTAN

"[Screenwriter Marshall Brickman] and I walk around the city. We review the experiences of my life. We talk about the ideas and feelings that are meaningful to us. It happens in an amorphous way. 'What if my ex-wife were writing a book about me?' Characters begin to appear; people I know, people we both know. Then others appear that are totally fabricated, sheer flights of fantasy."   —The New York Times Magazine, 1979

Complete the Quote and Name the Participants

Q1. "When it comes to relationships with women, I'm the winner of the _____ Award."

Q2. "That day at the planetarium, I was seized by a mad impulse to throw you down on the lunar surface and commit _____."

Q3. "I think people should mate for life, like _____."

Q4. "You're gonna leave Emily, to run away with the winner of the _____ Award?"

Q5. "My problem is, I'm both attracted and repelled by _____."

Courtesy of United Artists Pictures, Inc.

"Behind his black-rimmed glasses was the coiled sexual power of a jungle cat. New York was his town. And it always would be."   —*Isaac Davis*, Manhattan

. . .

Many people who've lived in New York all their lives did not recognize the city in *Manhattan*. Possibly, it had something to do with the lush black-and-white photography, or the Gershwin score, or the absence of muggers, subways, and garbage. In any event . . . how well do *you* know the city from the film?

. . .

311. *Manhattan* begins with a series of shots of various New York landmarks. Which of the following was *not* shown?
   a) Whitney Museum
   b) Yankee Stadium
   c) Chrysler Building
   d) Delacorte Theater

312. Which New York political personality makes a cameo appearance at the Museum of Modern Art?
   a. Shirley Chisholm
   b. Bella Abzug
   c. Jackie Onassis
   d. Gloria Steinem

313. In one of the pinnacles of onscreen romanticism, Isaac and Mary (Diane Keaton) quietly greet the dawn to the strains of "Someone to Watch over Me" (see photo). Identify the bridge in the background.

314. At which pizzeria do Isaac and Tracy (Mariel Hemingway) share a meal?
   a. Famous Ray's
   b. John's
   c. Original Ray's
   d. Pizzeria Uno

315. Besides the MOMA, two other art museums were visited in the film. Which ones?
  a. the Metropolitan and the Guggenheim
  b. the Frick and the Whitney
  c. the Whitney and the Guggenheim
  d. the Metropolitan and the Frick

316. Describing his reaction to finding out his ex-wife left him for a lesbian, Isaac Davis notes to Mary: "I took it well under the circumstances." What, in fact, did he do?
  a. soiled their lingerie with pesticide
  b. tried to run them both over with a car
  c. hired a phony assassin to spray their bedroom with rubber bullets
  d. pushed a grapefruit in their faces

317. According to Mary, having a dog serves as a penis substitute. "I would think, in your case, a great dane," Isaac responds. What kind of dog does she have?
  a. poodle
  b. golden Labrador retriever
  c. german shepherd
  d. dachshund

318. What is the title of the short story Isaac wrote about his mother?
  a. "The Neurotic Nihilist"
  b. "The Chicken Soup Imperialist"
  c. "The Castrating Zionist"
  d. "The Socialist Queen"

319. "I've never had the wrong kind . . . my worst one was right on the money." What is Isaac referring to?
  a. orgasm
  b. clams casino
  c. a hit of cocaine
  d. french kiss

"Manhattanites," *from left*: Michael Murphy, Diane Keaton, Woody, and Mariel Hemingway. *Courtesy of Brian Hamill/Photoreporters*

320. What does Isaac claim to call his analyst?
a. Muammar
b. Donny
c. Dr. Chomsky
d. Putz

321. According to Jill (Meryl Streep), Isaac's ex-wife, she mentions at least one nice thing about him in her exposé on their marriage, entitled "Marriage, Divorce, and Selfhood." What is it?
a. He cried when he watched *Gone With the Wind*.
b. He took their son to the circus on Rosh Hashanah.
c. He took her to a gay bar on her birthday.
d. He made brownie cakes dressed in her negligee.

322. "She was a kindergarten teacher . . . she got into drugs, she moved to San Francisco, she went into est, became a Moonie . . . she's with the William Morris Agency now." Who is Isaac referring to?
a. his agent
b. Patricia Hearst

c. his first wife
d. his first girl friend

323. TRUE OR FALSE: Anne Byrne, wife of Dustin Hoffman
and the actress who played Yale's wife Emily in the movie, met
Woody Allen at a group therapy session.

*"They probably sit around on the floor with wine and cheese and
mispronounce allegorical and didacticism."* —Isaac Davis,
*imagining a night at the apartment of one of Mary's
overintellectualized colleagues*

. . .

In *Annie Hall*, Alvy Singer notes: "One thing about intellectuals,
they proved you can be absolutely brilliant and have no idea
what's going on." In *Manhattan*, they still don't.

. . .

324. Isaac is sadly amazed at Yale's (Michael Murphy's) and
Mary's "Academy of the Overrated," where names drop faster
than coins in a slot machine. One of the following however, was
not a member:
a. Gustav Mahler
b. Heinrich Böll
c. Isak Dinesen
d. Mozart

325. On a visit to the Whitney Museum, Isaac and Mary stare at
an impressive piece of sculpture. Echoing an earlier comment by
Mary, Isaac marvels at the sculpture's
a. celestial otherness
b. negative capability
c. phallic foresight
d. didactic dimension

326. "Nah, I can't name any of them," Isaac answers Mary, "and fortunately, they never come up in conversation." What can't he name?
a. the Seven Dwarfs
b. the victims of the Boston Strangler
c. the satellites of Saturn
d. the women of the Gambino family

327. Before sleeping with Mary, Isaac sighs, noting that he's never had a relationship that's lasted longer than the one between
a. Hitler and Eva Braun
b. Cher and Gregg Allman
c. Pierre and Margaret Trudeau
d. the Lone Ranger and Tonto

328. TRUE OR FALSE: It was Isaac who first introduced Yale to Mary.

329. "We're all just human beings, you know . . . you think you're God!" What is Isaac's response to his friend Yale's outburst, after Isaac confronts him over stealing Mary back?
a. "I can't argue with what women think!"
b. "I've always been an overachiever!"
c. "You should have seen me last night!"
d. "I gotta model myself after somebody!"

330. What do Willie Mays, Groucho Marx, Marlon Brando, the second movement of the *Jupiter* Symphony, and Cézanne's apples and pears have to do with *Manhattan*?

? 19

STARDUST MEMORIES

*"**I** caught a lot of hostile flak on that picture, the most I ever got in my life. But it's my own personal favorite of all my films. I think people made a perceptual error about it when it came out. They thought, He thinks we're schmucks because we like him and he doesn't return our affection. But the point of the picture was that there is this character who has wealth, fame . . . and he's totally miserable in spite of it."* —Moviegoer, *1985*

Complete the Quote and Name the Participants

Q1. "To you, I'm an atheist. To God, I'm _____."

Q2. "I'm a nobody with a one-line part and I managed to impress you by sitting around speed-reading _____."

Q3. "For years I thought the 'Goldberg Variations' were something Mrs. and Mrs. Goldberg tried _____."

Q4. "I can prove that if there's life anywhere else in the world, they will have a _____ economy."

Q5. I'm an honest believer in democracy. And I also think the _____ system can work."

331. What poster dominates Sandy Bates's bedroom wall?
a. the My-Lai massacre
b. naked children running from napalm in Saigon
c. Richard Nixon's resignation speech
d. Diane Keaton

332. At a press conference for his new film, Bates recalls the time he took existential philosophy at NYU. He claims he
a. never attended class and scored 100
b. knew every answer on the final exam and scored a 65
c. left all ten questions blank and scored 100
d. left five questions blank and scored with his professor

333. Besieged by autograph hounds and fans, Sandy is pitched a screenplay idea, which is
a. a comedy about the survivors of Auschwitz
b. a sci-fi version of the Manson killings
c. a comedy about the Guyana mass suicides
d. a romantic comedy about Senator Eugene McCarthy

334. "For two days out of thirty, she was stable," says Tony Roberts (playing himself). "Yeah, but what a two days!" Sandy responds. The character they are talking about is played by
a. Isabelle Adjani
b. Charlotte Rampling
c. Jessica Harper
d. Anne De Salvo

335. What does Sandy's cook burn in the oven, causing him enough aggravation to yell at her, "I don't eat rodent."
a. chicken
b. duck
c. rabbit
d. kidney

336. Who is the *first* person to mutter that he liked Sandy's "earlier, funnier movies"?

    a. a fan at the Stardust
    b. a studio executive
    c. an extraterrestrial
    d. Sandy himself

337. The actress in the picture at right plays one of Sandy's lovers
in *Stardust Memories*. She is the only French movie star to appear in a Woody Allen film, having scored an international success
with *Cousin, Cousine*. She is
    a. Marie-France Pisier
    b. Isabelle Adjani
    c. Marie-Christine Barrault
    d. Nathalie Baye

338. An old Brooklyn childhood friend of Sandy's, Jerry Abra-
hams, accosts Sandy in the Stardust lobby. Now a cab driver,
he's envious of Sandy's wealth and fame. Sandy, however, explains to Jerry he's just lucky to have been brought up in a culture
that needs humor and jokes. Had he been born _____ he'd be
out of work.
    a. an Apache Indian
    b. an aborigine
    c. a black dwarf
    d. a WASP

339. Suicide was not a middle-class alternative in Sandy's family,
he notes at one point, explaining that his mother was too busy
_____ to think about suicide.
    a. sewing together Avenue U and Nineteenth Street in
        Brooklyn
    b. ironing her children's hair
    c. running the boiled chicken through the deflavorizing ma-
        chine
    d. renewing her subscription to *Psychology Today*

340. As in *Annie Hall* with *The Sorrow and the Pity*, and *Manhattan* with *Grand Illusion*, characters in *Stardust Memories* are

Courtesy of United Artists Pictures, Inc.

Jessica Harper.
Courtesy of artist

affected by a European art film. What movie do Sandy and Daisy (Jessica Harper) go to see?
- a. *The Bicycle Thief*
- b. *The Seventh Seal*
- c. *La Dolce Vita*
- d. *Breathless*

341. In a conversation with Daisy, what does Sandy jokingly claim to do for laughs?
- a. dance with bag ladies in Central Park
- b. skip down Fifth Avenue dressed as a policeman
- c. perform the Heimlich maneuver on a loved one
- d. take go-cart rides in the supermarket

342. TRUE OR FALSE: Sandy's comment "That's more than they do on the West Side Highway" refers to dental work done on an old writer friend of his who can smile for the first time.

343. "They're like the Mafia . . . they only kill their own." What is Sandy referring to?
   a. lawyers
   b. writers
   c. parents
   d. intellectuals

344. Two film critics appear in *Stardust Memories*, one of whom held an identical kind of weekend seminar that served as the basis for Woody's movie. The two critics are
   a. Gene Siskel and Roger Ebert
   b. David Ansen and Pauline Kael
   c. Charles Champlin and Clive Barnes
   d. Judith Crist and Howard Kissel

"I thought maybe I should have another actor play the role, but I really didn't care how it was perceived. I wanted to do what I wanted to do, and I felt that someday when I'm not in the gossip columns, people will be able to see the film and judge it on its merits."   —Saturday Review, *1980*

? 20

SIDE EFFECTS
Fiction Collection No. 3

345. What were the last, enigmatic words of Sandor Needleman after being tapped on the head by a wrecking ball?
- a. "No thanks, I already own a penguin."
- b. "The chives are in my back right pocket."
- c. "Last month was not a day for cabbage soup."
- d. "Is the veal stew ready?"

346. "Your work and my work are very similar although I'm not exactly sure what your work is." Who reportedly wrote this to Needleman?
- a. Adolf Hitler
- b. Billie Holiday
- c. Albert Einstein
- d. Orville Wright

347. TRUE OR FALSE: In "The Condemned," Juliet, Cloquet's Marxist girl friend, is one of the few women he knew who could hold two disparate concepts in her mind at once: the Hegelian dialectic, and why if you stick your tongue in a man's ear while he's making a speech he will begin to sound like Idi Amin.

348. Cloquet is mistakenly arrested for the murder of Gaston Brisseau. But he doesn't help his cause any. In addition to having his fingerprints discovered, he also makes the mistake of
    a. giving Brisseau a shampoo and blow dry
    b. signing the guestbook
    c. reading Brisseau a fairy tale while under surveillance
    d. paying Brisseau's phone bill

349. The following incident was *not* reported by an observer in "The UFO Menace."
    a. a huge white saucer instructed a man to call his service, where he received a message telling him to forward his brother's mail to Neptune
    b. a large mechanical claw from a UFO snatched two pieces of chicken from a man's hand and quickly retreated (the air force only returned one piece)
    c. a fiery winged creature sang "I've Got You Under My Skin" in Japanese
    d. a cigar-shaped object tailed its subject relentlessly, until it turned out to be his nose

350. In "The Kugelmass Episode" (cited by Woody as an inspiration for the film *The Purple Rose of Cairo*), Kugelmass is transported by his magician friend Persky into *Madame Bovary*, where he begins a love affair with Emma. But he insists on always arriving before page 120, because
    a. his attention span begins to wander after that
    b. he wants to avoid the quarrel between Emma and her husband on page 150
    c. he's scared he'll wind up in the book's appendix
    d. he wants to have Emma before she meets Rodolphe

351. After his affair with Emma ends, Kugelmass asks to be transported into *Portnoy's Complaint*, but disaster occurs, and he instead finds himself running for his life in
    a. *The Joy of Gay Sex*
    b. *Tasteless Jokes, Volume III*

   c. *Remedial Spanish*
   d. *The Memoirs of Richard Nixon*

352. In "My Speech to the Graduates," modern man is defined
as "Any man born after Nietzsche's edict that God is dead, but
before _____."
   a. Sid Caesar's "Your Show of Shows"
   b. the hit recording "I Wanna Hold Your Hand"
   c. video cassette recorders
   d. the birth of Michael Jackson

353. The speaker of "My Speech to the Graduates" predicts that
by 1990 _____ will be the dominant mode of social interaction.
   a. kidnapping
   b. coughing
   c. killing
   d. salivating

354. In "Reminiscences: Places and People," W. Somerset Maugham
notes how he brooded after a critic assailed his first short
story . . . though after giving it some thought, Maugham realized
the critic was right. He never forgot the incident and, years later,
   a. guided to the critic's farm a team of Nazi storm troopers
      who were looking for a house to occupy
   b. shone a light on the critic's house while the Luftwaffe
      was bombing London
   c. put a For Sale sign on the critic's house while the critic
      was overseas during World War II
   d. sent a note to the critic's wife that said her husband had
      contracted a rare social disease while enjoying a furlough
      in North Africa

335. According to Willard Pogrebin, narrator of "Nefarious Times
We Live In," he tried to assassinate Gerald Ford because
   a. a busty Yale co-ed wouldn't see him anymore unless he
      did it for her
   b. Ford had made nasty remarks to him years earlier on a

sandlot baseball diamond, when the president was known as Smoky Joe Finkelstein
- c. Ford had asked Pogrebin to follow him around the country and fire shots at him, being careful to miss
- d. he confused the president with Henry Ford, of the Ford Motor Company

356. The bullet, however, missed, lodging instead
- a. in the hatpin of a Rockette
- b. in some bratwurst at Himmelstein's Sausage Emporium
- c. in a vat of cheesecake at Lindy's
- d. in the nose of a tuba player in the Marching Band of the Virgin Mary

357. In "A Giant Step for Mankind," the narrator reveals a diary in which three scientists almost scooped Dr. Heimlich on his manuever to aid choking victims. At one point, they experiment with mice, inducing strangulation by
- a. coaxing one to open its mouth and then hurling pieces of steak down its throat
- b. coaxing it to hyperventilate while eating a veal chop
- c. coaxing it to munch brownies while giggling
- d. coaxing it to ingest healthy portions of Gouda cheese and making it laugh

358. What is Abraham Lincoln's answer to the farmer's question of "How long should a man's leg be?" which poses a good deal of trouble in "The Query"?
- a. long enough to reach his torso
- b. long enough to reach his wife
- c. long enough to reach the ground
- d. long enough to win the exacta at Belmont

359. Woody Allen won the O. Henry Award for Best Short Story, 1977, for the following story found in *Side Effects*:
- a. "The Kugelmass Episode"
- b. "Retribution"

   c. "The Shallowest Man"
   d. "My Apology"

360. What is slightly unusual about the two women Harold Cohen finds himself in love with in "Retribution"?
   a. They are mother and daughter.
   b. They are lesbian lovers.
   c. They are aunt and uncle.
   d. They are both Harold's first cousins.

21

A MIDSUMMER NIGHT'S SEX COMEDY

"I've always felt—and tried to express this in my films, that it's reasonable to believe there's more to life than meets the eye. I didn't want to get into it in a heavy and deep way, but I did want to suggest it, and of course around that period—1905—that kind of thinking was very much in the air."

—American Classic Screen, *1982*

Complete the Quote and Name the Participants

Q1. "Sex alleviates tension. Love _____."

Q2. "Marriage is _____."

Q3. "The saddest thing in life is _____."

361. TRUE OR FALSE: The rich classical music that provides the vibrant soundtrack to *A Midsummer Night's Sex Comedy* is by Mendelssohn.

A Day in the Country.
From the rear to the front: Julie Haggerty,
Tony Roberts, and Jose
Ferrer; Woody and
Mary Steenburgen.
*Courtesy of AP/Wide
World Photos*

362. What is Andrew's reaction when his wife Adrian (Mary
Steenburgen) first tells him that Ariel Wayman (Mia Farrow) will
be spending a weekend at the house with her fiancé?

    a. He laughs aloud in glee.
    b. He breaks a glass in the sink.
    c. He vigorously denies knowing her.
    d. He takes out an old scrapbook of photos.

363. Where did the forward-thinking Dulcy (Julie Haggerty) lose
her virginity?

    a. in a hammock
    b. on board the *Orient Express*
    c. in a swimming pool
    d. on the beach

364. How many contraceptives has Dr. Maxwell (Tony Roberts)
brought with him, in anticipation of his weekend with Dulcy?

    a. none
    b. fifteen
    c. five hundred
    d. three hundred

365. Mourning his missed opportunity to sleep with Ariel many
years ago, at a time when she was very promiscuous, Andrew
notes that she even slept with

    a. the string section of the New York Philharmonic
    b. the staff of the Four Seasons restaurant
    c. the entire infield of the Chicago White Sox
    d. the crew of the America's Cup yachting team

366. Andrew comes back from his afternoon walk with Ariel, but his wife hasn't even started dinner. Why?
    a. She's never made trout.
    b. She's been asking Dulcy how to please her husband in bed.
    c. She's been spying on Andrew.
    d. She engaged in group sex with Dulcy, Maxwell, and Leopold (Jose Ferrer).

367. "I could feel her lips tremble with feeling." Who says this, and why?
    a. Dulcy, realizing with a shock she's attracted to Ariel
    b. Leopold, after making a pass at Adrian
    c. Maxwell, after trying to kiss Ariel
    d. Andrew, after kissing Ariel

368. What is happening in another room while Leopold sings "The Lord's Prayer" at the piano?
    a. Everyone is attacking everybody else; Leopold doesn't even realize he's alone.
    b. Maxwell is trying to kill himself in the barn.
    c. Ariel is praying for Andrew to come seduce her.
    d. Adrian is attacking Andrew on the kitchen table.

369. What is Andrew's wedding present to Leopold and Ariel?
    a. an apparatus that removes the bones from fish
    b. a flying bicycle-plane
    c. a talking pacemaker
    d. an automatic toilet flusher

370. What sexual position does Adrian want to show Andrew as the film reaches its happy conclusion?

Leopold and Dulcy get
to know each other.
*Courtesy of AP/Wide
World Photos*

    a. the Velvet Buzzsaw
    b. the Chicken-Leg Squeeze
    c. the Mexican Cartwheel
    d. the Detroit Doorjamb

371. What is Maxwell's "dying" confession?
    a. He hates Ariel.
    b. He never got to sleep with Dulcy.
    c. He slept with Leopold.
    d. He slept with Adrian.

372. TRUE OR FALSE: Leopold dies making love to Ariel on
their wedding night.

373. How did Maxwell and Adrian first know there was an attraction between them?
    a. She went weak in the knees when he smelled her per-
       fume.
    b. She got excited giving him mouth-to-mouth after he
       choked on a mushroom.
    c. She broke into hiccups when he took his shirt off.
    d. She had an enormous appetite at dinner.

374. For all the lecherous goings-on, there are only two instances
of lovemaking during the movie. Who are the two couples?
   a. Maxwell and Ariel, Andrew and Dulcy
   b. Leopold and Dulcy, Andrew and Adrian
   c. Andrew and Ariel, Leopold and Dulcy
   d. Maxwell and Adrian, Andrew and Dulcy

22

ZELIG

"I thought that desire not to make waves, carried to an extreme, could lead to traumatic consequences. It could lead to a conformist mentality and ultimately, fascism. That's why I had to use the documentary form; I wouldn't want to see this character's private life." —The New York Times, *1963*

375. "Zelig" in Yiddish means
- a. transparent
- b. blessed
- c. neurotic
- d. quixotic

376. In the opening shot of the movie, Leonard Zelig is seen with
- a. Herbert Hoover
- b. Charles Lindbergh
- c. Al Jolson
- d. Franklin Delano Roosevelt

377. Zelig is first placed in the hospital after
- a. transforming from a Chinese to a Caucasian
- b. transforming from an Indian to a black man

c. tranforming from an Italian to a fat man

d. transforming from a German to a Greek

378. Which of the following intellectuals are seen in on-camera interviews?

a. Susan Sontag, William Styron, Carl Jung, Saul Bellow

b. Bruno Bettelheim, Irving Howe, Saul Bellow, Susan Sontag

c. Calvin Turner, Irwin Shaw, Carl Jung, Jonas Salk

d. Saul Bellow, Seymour Hersh, Bruno Bettelheim, Arthur Miller

379. Recounting his time as psychiatrist, Zelig notes that he and Freud broke over the concept of penis envy because

a. Zelig thought it should be limited to children

b. Freud thought it should be limited to animals

c. Freud thought it should be limited to women

d. Zelig thought it should be limited to Greeks

380. The name of the fictional 1935 Warner Brothers film made about Zelig's life is

a. *The Charming Chameleon*

b. *The Changing Man*

c. *The Wizard of Personality*

d. *Dizzying Heights*

381. What was Morris's deathbed advice to his son?

a. change personalities constantly

b. become an exterminator

c. commit suicide

d. save string

382. What happens to Dr. Bersky, after pronouncing that Zelig has a brain tumor?

a. He is hailed as a genius by the AMA.

b. He dies of a brain tumor two weeks later.

c. He is arrested for malpractice.

d. He operates on Zelig, who has developed one after the announcement.

Leonard Zelig, flanked by Calvin
Coolidge and Herbert Hoover. *Cour-*
tesy of Orion-Warner Company

"While you could say Zelig was blessed with a certain talent, that didn't mean he was a better human being."

—The New York Times, *1983*

383. According to his sessions with Dr. Eudora Fletcher (Mia Farrow), what was the first instance of Zelig changing his personality to fit the crowd he was with?
   a. when he turned Irish in a bar because he wasn't wearing green
   b. when he turned Italian in a pizzeria because he didn't have a gun
   c. when he turned Chinese at karate class because he didn't know kung-fu
   d. when he turned into a woman in a department store because he wasn't pregnant

384. While under observation in the hospital, Zelig is given somadril hydrate, an experimental drug that makes him
   a. climb the walls
   b. swivel his head
   c. eat his bed sheets
   d. all of the above

385. TRUE OR FALSE: Leonard Zelig is seen on a huge Times Square billboard smoking Camel cigarettes.

386. Why couldn't Cole Porter finish a song about Zelig, after writing the first line, "You're the tops . . . you're Leonard Zelig"?
   a. He realized how faddish and inconsequential Zelig is.
   b. Zelig heard the song and demanded that Porter stop it at once.
   c. He couldn't find anything that rhymes with "Zelig."
   d. Zelig was deemed insane and Porter didn't want to glorify him.

387. After being in the care of his half sister Ruth and her boyfriend, Zelig is abandoned by them when they are all shot to death. He disappears. Where is he finally discovered?

  a. in bed with Louise Brooks
  b. on-deck at Yankee Stadium, as Lou Zelig
  c. playing trumpet in a club with Louis Armstrong
  d. standing with Pope Pius on Easter Sunday at St. Peter's

"I wish we could put Woody into more shots with people speaking, but we just had too much trouble finding shots he could be inserted into. . . . We needed enough room, we needed a reason for him to be standing there, and we needed to be sure that no one walked in front of him" —Editor Susan Morse, on the technical complexities of making Zelig, The New York Times, *1983*

"You can't imagine how many crates of film we accumulated."
—Cinematographer Gordon Willis

388. After Zelig runs away from the bigamy scandal he's involved in, Dr. Fletcher, many months later, sees him in newsreel footage, next to Hitler at a rally. What is the name of the newsreel?
  a. *National Socialism: The Dread Evil*
  b. *National Socialists on the Rise*
  c. *National Socialists on the March*
  d. *National Socialists and What's Happening*

389. In one of the film's more complicated maneuvers, Woody, through the use of fifty-year-old lenses and modern-day mattes for lighting, is inserted into the on-deck circle at a baseball diamond, while _____ bats.
  a. Babe Ruth
  b. Lou Gehrig
  c. Honus Wagner
  d. Darryl Strawberry

390. According to the narrator, fascism was a perfect outlet for Zelig because it offered
  a. anonymity
  b. the opportunity for head bashing

Zelig with Dr. Eudora Fletcher.
Courtesy of Orion-Warner Company

c. redemption

d. German women

391. Zelig and Dr. Fletcher eventually escape the Nazis, and Zelig becomes an American hero once more, after setting a record for

a. swimming across the Atlantic Ocean, nonstop, via dog paddling

b. flying nonstop across the Atlantic in a balloon

c. flying nonstop across the Atlantic in a plane, upside down

d. flying across the Atlantic in a helicopter, with a stop for duty-free shopping in Shannon, Ireland

23

BROADWAY DANNY ROSE

"We eat in an uptown Italian restaurant very frequently, and the owner is a woman with blond hair and black glasses, constantly smoking a cigarette. She's great. And we'd go there, and Mia would say, 'Jeez, someday I would love to play that character.' Then I wrote the story. It's funny—when I presented her with the script, she said, 'I can't play this.' " —Moviegoer, 1985

392. "They tried two men sent over by the casting office for the part of the counterman. After the first one read his lines, Woody said, 'No!' The second one, Woody said, 'No!' Woody is a genius, a perfectionist, so I said, 'Woody, I can do better than that. I'm a member of the Screen Actors Guild.' " The man who said this is Leo Steiner, co-owner of the deli where parts of *Broadway Danny Rose* were shot (see photo on page 152): Which deli was it?

    a. Second Avenue Deli
    b. Katz's Deli
    c. Carnegie Deli
    d. Stage Deli

The Carnegie Deli. *Courtesy of Todd Lane*

393. Danny Rose handles an incredible variety of eccentric clients. One of them, in real life, is the part she plays. Which client in the movie is this?
   a. a one-legged tap dancer
   b. a blind xylophone player
   c. a one-armed juggler
   d. a glasspiel

394. Another of Danny's clients is a parrot who sings
   a. "Strangers in the Night"
   b. "In the Mood"
   c. "Jailhouse Rock"
   d. "I've Gotta Be Me"

395. "You can have him at the old price," Danny pleads, trying to sell his client to a club owner. What is the "old price"?
   a. $2.50
   b. anything he wants to give him
   c. $10
   d. $50

396. As the comedians exchange Danny Rose stories, one re-counts the time Danny's hypnotist could not snap a woman out of a trance. As the husband nervously stood by, Danny promised that, should the man's wife die, he will
a. take him to the restaurant of his choice
b. let him beat Danny up
c. match him up immediately with his sister
d. take her to a better hypnotist

397. Who looked like "something you'd buy in a live-bait shop"?
a. Uncle Rose
b. Aunt Rose
c. Danny's ex-wife
d. Danny's cousin, Celia

398. Jack Rollins and Charles Joffe, Woody's managerial team, were involved in *Broadway Danny Rose* beyond their normal roles as producers. How?
a. Charles Joffe was an extra at the Italian wedding.
b. Jack Rollins played one of the comics.
c. Both Rollins and Joffe were extras at the wedding.
d. Both Rollins and Joffe played comics.

"While we were making the movie, I said to him: 'Wood, I can't put you on. I've never seen one of your movies in my life.' And he says to me, 'You are a very disturbed individual.' "
—*Nick Apollo Forte, The New York Times, 1984*

399. TRUE OR FALSE: Nick Apollo Forte (his middle name is derived from New York's Apollo Theater), a cocktail pianist who had never acted in his life, was discovered when one of Woody Allen's casting agents found a copy of Forte's album, *Images,* which he had released under his *own* label, in a Broadway store.

400. Whose talk show does Lou Canova (Forte) make an ap-pearance on?

Danny Rose hard at
work as Lou Canova's
"Beard." *Courtesy of
Brian Hamill/Photo-
reporters*

    a. David Letterman's
    b. Merv Griffin's
    c. Jack Paar's
    d. Joe Franklin's

401. When we first hear Tina (Mia Farrow), the girl Lou Canova
is crazy about, she's
    a. on the phone with Lou, telling him to drop dead
    b. getting her fortune read by a psychic
    c. eating with Lou, trying to get him to change managers
    d. making anti-Semitic remarks to Danny

*"**I** didn't know if I could do it . . . it was such a different character, and I wasn't sure how I would get there or anything."*
                           —*Mia Farrow, commenting on the part*
                              of Tina, The New York Times, *1984*

402. How does Tina's jilted Italian lover Johnny confuse Danny
with Lou as the man Tina is leaving him for?
    a. Someone's been sending Tina Broadway show tickets,
       and Danny Rose's nickname is "Broadway" Danny.

   b. Someone's been serenading Tina with love songs, and
      Danny used to be a singer.
   c. Someone's been sending Tina mash notes and signing
      them "Danny."
   d. Someone's been sending Tina a white rose a day, and
      Danny's last name is Rose.

403. What does a despairing Johnny finally do, in front of the
entire family?
   a. stab himself
   b. drinks iodine
   c. hangs himself from the balcony
   d. reads a poem in Italian ordering Danny's death

404. What business is Tina's Uncle Rocco in?
   a. cement
   b. loan-sharking
   c. prostitution
   d. television

405. When Johnny's Italian brothers find Danny and Tina at a
New Jersey diner, Tina leads Danny out the back door, knowing
they want to kill him. What does she say to him that convinces
him to climb into the weeds and muck off the road?
   a. "They'll rip your tongue out of your head."
   b. "They'll castrate you and then torture you."
   c. "You'll wind up on a meathook."
   d. "You'll wind up without a throat."

406. Barney Dunn is the poor, innocent guy fingered by Danny
as Tina's lover when Danny is protecting Lou Canova (and himself) from getting knocked off by the crazed brothers. What was
Barney known as?
   a. the world's best flasher
   b. the world's oldest virgin
   c. the world's worst ventriloquist
   d. the world's worst lover

24

THE PURPLE ROSE
OF CAIRO

"This was just a funny notion that occurred to me one day, and within forty-eight hours all the developments fell into place. I got the notion of a character slipping down off the screen, and I thought that was fun to play with. I felt that it could be amusing and romantic . . . and I also felt there could be something to say in the picture."
—Moviegoer, 1985

Complete the Quote and Name the Participants

Q1. "You can't learn to be real . . . it's like learning to be a _____."

Q2. "I just met a wonderful new man. He's a _____, but you can't have everything."

Q3. "Love at first sight doesn't happen just in _____."

407. What is the name of the theater where *The Purple Rose of Cairo* is playing?
   a. the Gem
   b. the Jewel

c. the Bijou
d. the Beekman

408. The characters in *Purple Rose* are planning a trip to
a. Morocco
b. Italy
c. Turkey
d. Mozambique

409. The legend of the Purple Rose is that
a. it grows on a tree once planted by Mohammed
b. it is responsible for the parting of the Red Sea
c. it turns anyone who looks at it purple
d. it grows, wild, on a queen's tomb

410. When the characters in the movie meet Tom Baxter (Jeff Daniels), "poet/adventurer/explorer of the Chicago Baxters," why do they take him back to New York to meet the Countess?
a. She wants to imprison him and torture him for hiding the Purple Rose.
b. She wants to marry off her daughter.
c. She likes anything in a pith helmet.
d. She likes anything in khaki.

"I had been out of Terms of Endearment *about a week or two, when my agent calls and says, 'You're not gonna believe this. You're going to meet Woody Allen tomorrow.' Juliet Taylor set it up. She said: 'Don't be upset. It's going to be two minutes.' I met Woody. He asked me, did I have time to stick around [New York] to read for a part. I said, sure."* —Jeff Daniels

411. Jeff Daniels was not originally slated to play Gil/Tom. In desperation Woody almost rewrote the part for himself, after the original actor proved too "contemporary" for the role. Who was he?
a. Michael Keaton

Jeff Daniels (*above*) and
Danny Aiello (*left*). *Courtesy
of artists*

  b. Tom Hanks
  c. Gene Wilder
  d. Ron Silver

412. How many times does Cecilia (Mia Farrow) see the movie before Tom Baxter steps off the screen?
  a. five
  b. four
  c. ten
  d. twice

413. Why hasn't Tom Baxter ever met his father?
  a. He died before the movie begins.
  b. He was written out of the script before Tom meets him.
  c. His father never wanted to meet Tom, since he thought *he* should be playing Tom's part.
  d. His father appears at the very end of the movie, which Tom is not in.

414. What role is Gil Shepherd supposed to play after Tom Baxter?
  a. Napoleon
  b. F. Scott Fitzgerald
  c. Jack Dempsey
  d. Charles Lindbergh

415. Why is Tom so puzzled when he first kisses Cecilia?
  a. She resists, which no one ever does in the movies.
  b. He can't feel his lips.
  c. He expects a fade-out, like in the movies.
  d. She turns into the character he's supposed to meet in the film's next reel, and he despises her.

416. Who does Tom think created the world?
  a. God
  b. Irving Saks and R. H. Levine, screenwriters of *The Purple Rose*
  c. Gil Shepherd, the actor who plays him
  d. Cecilia

Tom Baxter discovers real life, assisted by a few ladies of the night.
Courtesy of Brian Hamill/Photoreporters

417. How come the rest of the actors in *Purple Rose* cannot step off the screen as Tom Baxter can?
    a. It's against union rules.
    b. They are repelled by electrical shocks.
    c. They can, but they're more fascinated with their movie.
    d. This is never adequately explained.

418. Once Cecilia is taken into the movie by Tom, she is thrown into the Copacabana scene, where she is surprised to find that
    a. the champagne bottles are filled with ginger ale
    b. the check is paid with Monopoly money
    c. the actors all have to hit marks
    d. Tom Baxter is supposed to marry Kitty Haines (Deborah Rush)

419. After being taken to a brothel (see photo), Tom Baxter politely resists the ladies' carnal offers, despite the fact that they are so taken with him they offer to do him for free! How can he resist?
   a. He's a movie character, and he's never made love.
   b. He is afraid to hurt Gil Shepherd's career.
   c. He loves Cecilia too much.
   d. He's a closet homosexual.

420. The talented Baxter serenades Cecilia on a musical instrument. Which one does he play?
   a. clarinet
   b. ukulele
   c. harmonica
   d. flute

421. Which Fred Astaire movie is Cecilia unhappily watching at the end of the movie, after Gil has flown off to California?
   a. *Top Hat*
   b. *Singin' in the Rain*
   c. *Damsel in Distress*
   d. *The Road to Morocco*

"In life, you can't really choose fantasy, because if you do, you're very limited. Mia's character can only have a life with this movie hero in a strange, limited way. In real life, people disappoint you. They're cruel, and life is cruel. And if you choose reality over fantasy, which you must—you have to pay the price for it."
                                              —Moviegoer, *1985*

25

HANNAH AND HER SISTERS

"At first, the film had a simple single plot about a man who falls in love with his wife's sister. Then, the summer before last, I reread Anna Karenina, *and I thought, It's interesting how this guy gets the various stories going, cutting from one story to another. I loved the idea of experimenting with that."*
—The New York Times, *1986*

Complete the Quote and Name the Participants

Q1. "We did everything but _____."

Q2. "I had a great time. It was like _____."

Q3. "The heart is a very, very _____ little muscle."

Q4. "Her father could be anyone in _____."

"I have a tremendous attraction to movies or plays or books that explore the psyches of women, particularly intelligent ones."
—The New York Times, *1986*

Frederick (Max von Sydow) is not thrilled at what Dusty (Daniel Stern) considers art.
Courtesy of Brian Hamill/Photoreporters

422. In what famous play has Hannah (Mia Farrow) just completed a successful acting run?

    a. *The Three Sisters*
    b. *The Glass Menagerie*
    c. *A Doll's House*
    d. *You Can't Take It with You*

423. When we first meet Woody as Mickey Sachs, the hypochondriac producer, a sketch on his TV show is being censored. "Half the country is doing it!" Mickey gripes. What is the sensitive subject under dispute?

    a. child molesting
    b. masturbation
    c. necrophilia
    d. income-tax evasion

424. TRUE OR FALSE: Hannah never finds out about the affair between her husband, Elliot (Michael Caine), and her sister Lee (Barbara Hershey).

425. After finding out he doesn't have a brain tumor, Mickey bursts out of the hospital, jumping for joy. Why does he suddenly stop?

    a. He realizes he forgot to tell the doctor about the lump on his leg.

The Pageant Book & Print Shop, where Elliot and Lee discussed Cara-
vaggio while thinking other things. *Courtesy of Todd Lane*

  b. He realizes how much money he's spent for nothing.
  c. He realizes that eventually, he's still going to die.
  d. He runs into his ex-wife.

426. What is the name of the rock group that Hannah's sister
Holly (Dianne Wiest) drags Mickey to (at CBGB!) on their ill-
fated first date?
  a. the Sick Fucks
  b. the 39 Steps
  c. Rear Entry
  d. the Maniacs

427. While being driven home by the architect whom both April
(Carrie Fisher) and Holly are competing for, a disgruntled Holly
sits in the backseat, wondering how April came up with the phrase
organic quality, while talking about buildings. "Of course," Holly
grumbles,
  a. "she took art history at the New School."

Sam Waterston.
Courtesy of artist

   b. "she eats organic food."
   c. "she's an organic bitch."
   d. "she went to Brandeis."

428. After leaving his job to search for Meaning, Mickey decides Catholicism is the answer. He observes priests in action, and is soon taken with Catholic fever. He comes home and unloads a shopping bag containing
   a. Hellmann's, Wonder Bread, a Bible, a cross, and a picture of Mary
   b. Wonder Bread, a picture of Mary, pastrami, a shawl, and a cross
   c. the Old Testament, Hellmann's, a picture of Jesus, and a huge ham
   d. a cross, Heinz ketchup, the New Testament, and dill pickles

429. Still searching desperately for Answers, Mickey confronts his parents over how, if God exists, he could allow Nazis. What is Mickey's father's reaction?

Max von Sydow, Woody's first actor from the Bergman repertory company. *Courtesy of artist*

   a. "He allowed New Jersey, didn't he?"
   b. "How should I know? I don't even know how the can opener works."
   c. "What was so bad about Nazis . . . till they got a little carried away?"
   d. "What difference does it make now? I gotta take a dump."

430. Where does Mickey run into Holly, years after their first date?
   a. a halfway house
   b. Carnegie Hall
   c. Rizzoli's bookstore
   d. Tower Records

431. "We need some sperm." Who says this, and why?
   a. the hare krishnas, to Mickey, in order for him to begin practicing with them
   b. the Stanislavski Catering Company, on the day they cater an orgy

    c. Mickey, to his writing partner, in a flashback to Mickey
       and Hannah's marriage, right after Mickey has found out
       he's infertile
    d. Elliot and Hannah, to a doctor, worried about Elliot's
       sudden impotence

432. Of Mia Farrow's eight children, how many appeared in *Hannah and Her Sisters*?
    a. seven
    b. six
    c. two
    d. four

433. After taking a long, dazed walk through city streets, Mickey
is finally convinced that the world is not such a bad place to live.
How does he realize this?
    a. he gets mugged
    b. he's entertained by a Marx Brothers movie
    c. he's captivated by the World Series on television in a bar
    d. he watches a shootout between police and a bank robber

*"The overview is how silly and sad and endearing we are for
being so involved in all these relationships when really we're
going to die. And yet, what else are we going to do?"*
             —*Barbara Hershey,* The New York Times, *1986*

26

RADIO DAYS

"It was an extremely romantic time in the United States. The popular culture of the day was movies and radio, and it was a very glamorous age. Radio had a tremendous hold on the nation . . . families gathered together in the evening, and those wonderful stories were coming over the air . . . I would present the argument that it was just a more charming time and a better time." —The New York Times, *1987*

434. At the beginning of the film, two burglars are robbing the Needlemans' house at night when they are interrupted by a call from the radio show "Guess That Tune." After two correct answers, the burglars win the jackpot when they guess the third song. What is the song?
   a. "Dancing in the Dark"
   b. "The Sailor's Hornpipe"
   c. "Chinatown, My Chinatown"
   d. "Stormy Weather"

435. Playing the young Woody Allen character (Joe), Seth Green gets in trouble at a class show-and-tell session. What does he display?

a. a pistol
b. a pair of panties
c. a tampon
d. a condom

436. Aunt Bea (Dianne Wiest) goes out on a date with a man she has a crush on, Sidney Manulis. But the evening ends in disaster. When he calls her for a date the following week, she instructs her mother to tell him that she can't see him anymore, because
a. she prefers women
b. she married a Martian
c. she swallowed a giant filet
d. she wants to rip out his spleen

437. Sally White, the cocktail waitress (Mia Farrow) who dreams of becoming an actress, finally gets her big chance to be a radio star after she narrowly escapes being rubbed out by a Mafia assassin. Unfortunately, as Woody notes in his narration, the world never gets to hear her voice. Minutes before she is to debut on a radio drama, what happens?
a. the Japanese bombed Pearl Harbor
b. she got permanent laryngitis
c. Orson Welles's "War of the Worlds" sent everyone into a panic
d. the *Hindenburg* exploded

438. Uncle Abe, indignant over the Waldbaums' indifference to Yom Kippur, the Jewish holy day, goes next door to straighten them out. But he comes back home with a distinct change in attitude. He is now
a. a proponent of free love
b. espousing Communist work ethics
c. eating Communion wafers
d. a fascist sympathizer

439. Prior to being run over by a truck, Kirby Kyle, the courageous baseball pitcher featured on Bill Kern's "Famous Sports

Legends," displays rare courage and heart, after being crippled in a string of hunting accidents. The accidents leave Kirby pitching

    a. with one arm, two legs, and one ear
    b. deaf, with no arms and one leg
    c. with one arm, no legs, and two hands
    d. blind, with one arm and one leg

440. The Waldbaums are upset when Cousin Ruthie snoops on their phone conversation. What does she overhear?

    a. that Mr. Waldbaum has been arrested for statutory rape
    b. that Mrs. Waldbaum is having her ovaries removed
    c. that Mr. Waldbaum's son sleeps with animals
    d. all of the above

441. Why are Joe and a few of his friends enthralled in class by a substitute teacher, Miss Gordon?

    a. Their regular teacher is a Nazi.
    b. They've seen her dancing naked in front of a mirror.
    c. They've seen her making love to the principal.
    d. She's not wearing a bra.

442. Early in the movie, Joe is beaten simultaneously by the rabbi, his mother, and his father after he is caught trying to raise money to buy the Masked Avenger's secret-compartment ring. How was he trying to raise the money?

    a. by collecting donations for a Jewish homeland in Palestine
    b. by trying to act as a gigolo for rich Jewish women
    c. by selling a package of Torahs as "encyclopedias"
    d. by trying to start his own radio show, "Famous Jewish Hockey Stars"

443. Match Woody's childhood memory to the song associated with it:

1. sees parents kiss for the first time	a. "If I Didn't Care" b. "You and I"

2. Mr. Zipsky's nervous breakdown, during which he swings a meat cleaver at the neighbors
3. schoolmates enhance a snowman's anatomy with a carrot
4. is taken to Radio City Music Hall for the first time
5. breaks down resistance of a shy girl, Evelyn Goorwitz

c. "Paper Doll"
d. "Pistol Packin' Mama"
e. "Mairzy Doats"

"The whole country was tied together by radio. We all experienced the same heroes and comedians and singers. They were giants. They were so huge and now today the whole thing has completely vanished. It's very sobering. There was just nobody bigger when I grew up than some of these people. . . . We think we have such a hold on the public and then with the passage of time, it all gets dissipated."   —The New York Times, *1987*

27

GIRLS, GIRLS, GIRLS
The Women in
Woody's Films

"I don't see myself as a Woody Allen actress. I don't think that's my role in life. But then, you know, it's been great being in his movies. I have difficulty in expressing myself—obviously—and I'm a clown in some ways." —Diane Keaton, Time Out, *1977*

"He knows what I can and can't do maybe better than I do myself. When you're working with someone you're so close to, you don't want to disappoint them—you feel you just must do it."
—Mia Farrow, The New York Times, *1984*

444. Between them, Diane Keaton and Mia Farrow have been in twelve of Woody Allen's movies, appearing together for the first time in *Radio Days*. Which ones did *neither* actress appear in?
   a. *Interiors, Stardust Memories*
   b. *Everything You Always Wanted to Know About Sex . . . , Take the Money and Run, Stardust Memories*
   c. *Sleeper, The Purple Rose of Cairo, Broadway Danny Rose*
   d. *Take the Money and Run, Zelig, A Midsummer Night's Sex Comedy*

445. At one point, Diane had to switch from an intense role in
another movie she was making to reshoot, on her off-day, the
ending for a Woody Allen film. What movie was Keaton working on?
   a. *The Godfather*
   b. *The Godfather, Part II*
   c. *Looking for Mr. Goodbar*
   d. *Shoot the Moon*

*"When we first met, we would go for long walks in the park and
talk about art and philosophy and life and all the things you
find out neither of you likes to do."*
                        —Louise Lasser, The New York Times, *1971*

446. Louise Lasser appeared in *Take the Money and Run*, *Bananas*, and *Everything You Always Wanted to Know About
Sex . . .* , not to mention a voice-over part in *What's Up, Tiger
Lily?* She also had a bit role as a secretary in another Allen film.
Which one?
   a. *Sleeper*
   b. *Stardust Memories*
   c. *Love and Death*
   d. *Zelig*

447. Before making her mark in movies, Louise Lasser was already known to American audiences in the mid-sixties (not nec-
essarily by name) as
   a. Agnes, a recurring guest on "The Flying Nun"
   b. Miss Catherine Thornhill, a merciless heiress on the CBS
      soap opera "As the World Turns"
   c. Mrs. Juliet Bedford, co-director of Sotheby's
   d. Mildred, the sympathetic housewife on a TV commercial
      for a popular cold remedy

448. "I saw some photos of her in *Interview* magazine and I
thought—and still do think—that she's probably the most beau-

tiful woman that the world has yet seen." Woody made these
comments prior to casting
   a. Marie-Christine Barrault in *Stardust Memories*
   b. Barbara Hershey in *Hannah and Her Sisters*
   c. Mariel Hemingway in *Manhattan*
   d. Mary Steenburgen in *A Midsummer Night's Sex Comedy*

449. Woody's fondness for women is apparent in his casting. Some
illustrious actresses have glided through his movies . . . ranging
from leading roles to silent walk-ons. Match them with their
movies:

1. Charlotte Rampling	a. *Interiors*
2. Meryl Streep	b. *Hannah and Her Sisters*
3. Julie Haggerty	c. *Stardust Memories*
4. Mary Beth Hurt	d. *Annie Hall*
5. Lynn Redgrave	e. *Manhattan*
6. Carrie Fisher	f. *Everything You Always Wanted to Know About Sex . . .*
7. Sigourney Weaver	g. *A Midsummer Night's Sex Comedy*

450. She plays a neurotic classical violinist with lesbian overtones
and Diane Keaton's Russian cousin in her only two Woody Allen
films, and was even linked romantically with Woody for a short
time. She is
   a. Jessica Harper
   b. Mary Steenburgen
   c. Janet Margolin
   d. Liv Ullmann

451. "When he finds something beautiful in a woman, he forces
the audience to see it, too." Which actress said this about Woody?
   a. Julie Haggerty
   b. Carrie Fisher
   c. Barbara Hershey
   d. Kristen Griffith

452. There are two actors whom Woody claims to have been "awed" by, one of them being Max von Sydow, who appears in *Hannah and Her Sisters*. Who is the other?
   a. Maureen Stapleton
   b. Lynn Redgrave
   c. Shelley Duvall
   d. Geraldine Page

453. "She's the only person I ever met who can cheer me up." Woody once said this about
   a. Mia Farrow
   b. Diane Keaton
   c. Louise Lasser
   d. Gilda Radner

"I've been crazy about the women I've acted with and I would be happy to end up as their chauffeur and housemaid. I don't mind that, with any of them. Answering her fan mail. Writing *her fan mail."*   —The New York Times, *1985*

28

I DON'T WANT TO ACHIEVE IMMORTALITY THROUGH MY WORK . . . I WANT TO ACHIEVE IT THROUGH NOT DYING

"You only have to be with him for a short while to appreciate that along with his work and Diane Keaton, his other favorite subject is the gloomiest of them all—death."
—*Frank Rich*, Esquire, *1977*

"Life is a concentration camp . . . you're stuck here, and there's no way out, and you can only rage impotently against your persecutors." —Esquire, *1977*

454. Who says, "I'm not afraid to die, I just don't want to be there when it happens"?
   a. Danny Rose in *Broadway Danny Rose*
   b. Nat Ackerman in *Death Knocks*
   c. Sandy Bates in *Stardust Memories*
   d. Kleinman in *Death*

455. The first book on death that Alvy Singer buys Annie Hall is
   a. *Death in Venice*
   b. *Death in the Afternoon*
   c. *Denial of Death*
   d. *Great Moments in Death*

456. In what movies does a Woody Allen character actually die?
    a. *Bananas, Sleeper*
    b. *Everything You Always Wanted to Know About*
       Sex . . . , Love and Death, Casino Royale
    c. *Sleeper, Stardust Memories, Love and Death*
    d. *A Midsummer Night's Sex Comedy, Zelig*

457. In which two films does an Allen character actually (albeit belatedly) attempt suicide?
    a. *Zelig, The Front*
    b. *Everything You Always Wanted to Know About*
       Sex . . . , Sleeper
    c. *Hannah and Her Sisters, Love and Death*
    d. *Bananas, Stardust Memories*

458. Which Allen character exclaims, "I can't do anything to the death . . . doctor's orders."
    a. Boris Grushenko
    b. Miles Monroe
    c. Fielding Mellish
    d. Leonard Zelig

459. Match these grim lines with the movies they were uttered in:

1. "I just wanna make sure when I thin out . . . that I'm well thought of."	a. *Annie Hall*
	b. *Stardust Memories*
	c. *Bananas*
2. "Think of death as a more effective way of cutting down your expenses."	d. *Manhattan*
	e. *Love and Death*
3. "I have been poisoned so many times I have developed an immunity."	
4. "I'm obsessed with death. It's a big subject with me."	
5. "I would trade that Oscar for one more second of life."	

Woody and friend. *Courtesy of United Artists Pictures, Inc.*

460. Generally, Woody has not succeeded in killing off the character he plays, but at the end of one movie, he not only winds up dead, but in hell to boot. Which one?
   a. *Love and Death*
   b. *Stardust Memories*
   c. *Casino Royale*
   d. none of the above

461. TRUE OR FALSE: Woody Allen characters twice face firing squads and escape both times.

462. Where is Mickey Sachs, in *Hannah and Her Sisters*, when he first learns that his symptoms could be the signs of a brain tumor?
   a. on the set of his TV show
   b. in a phone booth on Park Avenue
   c. in bed with a date
   d. walking in Central Park with a hare krishna

463. "There are worse things than death," says Boris Grushenko. "Anyone who's spent an evening with _____ knows exactly what I mean."
   a. a used-car salesman
   b. a foot doctor
   c. an English professor
   d. an insurance salesman

"I was watching Walt Frazier one night with the Knicks. He was so beautiful and young, so dazzling, but I saw the death's-head looming. I thought of the inevitable deterioration, the waning away of the adulation. I felt that anger and rage, not at anything correctable, but at the human condition that you're part of, too."
                                        —American Film, *1978*

29

ONE BIG HAPPY FAMILY

"While most commercial filmmakers in America go from one project to the other, hiring actors and technicians picture by picture, Mr. Allen adheres to another tradition: like Preston Sturges, he has developed a kind of repertory company for his films. . . ." —Janet Maslin, The New York Times, *1984*

. . .

(The actresses in this repertory company have already been honored with their own chapter. Even if you have cheated and read the chapters out of sequence, this chapter will still make perfect sense.)

. . .

"I never lived in Los Angeles, so if people think I'm dying to move out to L.A., I have Mr. Allen to thank. He likes to use me as his alter ego—the prototypical assimilated Jew. We made jokes that we were going to name A Midsummer Night's Sex Comedy, Two Jews in the Country.*"*

—Tony Roberts, On the Avenue, *1986*

Tony Roberts.
Courtesy of artist

464. Tony Roberts was the first leading actor to appear in both a Woody Allen play and film adaptation, playing Dick in both versions of *Play It Again, Sam*, as well as Axel Magee in *Don't Drink the Water*. (Jerry Lacy also played Bogart in both versions of *Sam*). Name the two actors who appeared in both an Allen play and a film directed by Allen.
  a. Gene Wilder and Jackie Gleason
  b. Danny Aiello and Lou Jacobi
  c. Jack Weston and Michael Murphy
  d. Brian Backer and Jeff Daniels

465. TRUE OR FALSE: Before collaborating for the first time on *Sleeper*, Woody Allen and Marshall Brickman co-wrote *The Filmmaker*, produced in 1971 by United Artists under an Allen pseudonym.

466. Prior to his collaborations with Brickman (*Sleeper*, *Annie Hall*, *Manhattan*), Woody Allen wrote which movie(s) with Mickey Rose, a childhood friend with whom he once planned to open an optometrist's shop?

a. *Take the Money and Run, Bananas*
b. *Take the Money and Run*
c. *Bananas*
d. *Take the Money and Run, Bananas, Everything You Always Wanted to Know About Sex . . .*

467. He scored Woody Allen's first two films, despite a less than enthusiastic introduction, when he was reportedly left weeping on a studio recording floor by Woody's passive reaction ("What was *that*?") to his demo tapes. Who is he?
a. Paul Simon
b. Mike Oldfield
c. Marvin Hamlisch
d. Dick Hyman

468. When Carlo Di Palma shot *Hannah and Her Sisters*, it marked the first time that Woody used a different cinematographer since *Annie Hall*, a run of eight pictures. Di Palma took the place of
a. Nestor Almendros
b. Michael Chapman
c. Sven Nykvist
d. Gordon Willis

469. Before Susan E. Morse became Woody's film editor, starting with *Manhattan* (she also assisted on *Annie Hall*), Ralph Rosenblum cut five of Woody's first six films, missing only
a. *Everything You Always Wanted to Know About Sex . . .*
b. *Love and Death*
c. *Sleeper*
d. *Bananas*

470. He is not an actor by trade, but has enjoyed bit roles in no less than *five* Woody Allen films, playing a Greek waiter in *Zelig*, an Armenian fan in *Stardust Memories*, a Porsche owner in *Manhattan*, a hotel manager in *Broadway Danny Rose*, and a coke fiend in *Annie Hall*. Being one of Woody's closest friends may have something to do with it. Who is he?

Woody's repertory company,
past and present: Editor Susan
E. Morse (*above, courtesy of
Barry Sonnenfeld*), Production
Designer Mel Bourne (*right,
courtesy of Kerry Hayes*)

Woody Allen on his
weekly Monday night
at Michael's Pub.
*Courtesy of UPI/
Bettman Newsphotos*

    a. Wallace Shawn
    b. Howard Cosell
    c. John Doumanian
    d. Ingmar Bergman

471. Woody has always managed to catch actors before they achieved runaway success, when any little cameo was gratefully appreciated. None other than Rocky/Rambo himself, otherwise known as Sylvester Stallone, can be glimpsed as a leather-jacketed hood in
    a. *Take the Money and Run*
    b. *Play It Again, Sam*
    c. *Bananas*
    d. *Sleeper*

472. TRUE OR FALSE: Howard Cosell, who acts in *Bananas*, has a brief cameo in *Broadway Danny Rose*, and is glimpsed on a TV screen in *Sleeper*, was supposed to play a sex pervert in *Everything You Always Wanted to Know About Sex . . .* , but turned it down for fear his image would suffer irreparable damage.

473. Woody has always had a profound appreciation for music, not only in the rich soundtracks of his movies, but also as a clarinet player himself. Woody once scored one of his movies, going down to New Orleans to record the soundtrack with the New Orleans Preservation Jazz Hall Band and the New Orleans Funeral Ragtime Orchestra, with whom he played clarinet. Which movie did he do this for?
  a. *Zelig*
  b. *Stardust Memories*
  c. *Sleeper*
  d. *The Purple Rose of Cairo*

474. She has cast every Woody Allen movie since *Annie Hall*, and is renowned for finding the weirdest, funniest, strangest, fattest, saddest faces in New York. (If you don't believe this, see *Stardust Memories*.) She is
  a. Joy Todd
  b. Juliet Taylor
  c. June Henderson
  d. Dorothy Parker

"Traditionally, we don't know what his movies are about. We will find out the cast when Woody decides to tell us."
  —Lloyd Leipzig, Orion vice-president of publicity, explaining Woody's degree of creative control to the New York Times, *1982*

"The transfer of my films from UA to Orion was effected for my own best interests. I lead exactly the same kind of life. I see the same friends, the same collaborators. I consider myself eminently privileged. I work as an independent, answerable to no one."   —In Robert Benayoun, The Films of Woody Allen, *1986*

30

IT'S NOT THE QUANTITY THAT COUNTS, BUT THE QUALITY

"I don't think of it as girl-chasing. . . . People are lonely, they have difficulties with women, sex is a great area of human concern. I'm trying to show a guy caught up in all that."
—Village Voice, *1976*

"One of the prison psychiatrists asked me if I thought sex was dirty, and I said it is if you're doing it right."
—*Virgil Starkwell*, Take the Money and Run

475. One of the funniest vignettes in Woody's stand-up routine is his graphic description of how he thinks about baseball players in order to sustain his sexual performance. This comes up in one film as well, when Woody's bedmate tells him, "I couldn't figure out why you kept yelling, 'Slide!' " Which Allen character is next to her?

a. Fielding Mellish
b. Victor Shakopopolis
c. Alvy Singer
d. Allan Felix

476. Woody, his girl friend, and a male friend are transported by the devil on a guided tour of hell's nine layers, Level 5 of which is for "organized crime, fascist dictators, and people who don't like oral sex." Unfortunately, this scene was excised, from
   a. *Annie Hall*
   b. *Manhattan*
   c. *Stardust Memories*
   d. *Hannah and Her Sisters*

477. Masturbation may not be the dominant theme of Woody's work, but it certainly has been good for its share of one-liners. Match the line to the film:

1. Don't knock masturbation . . . it's sex with someone I love.
2. Art and masturbation—two areas in which I am an absolute expert
3. Suppose he's masturbating? I'm liable to wind up on the ceiling!
4. It's an advanced class . . . if I'm late, my students start without me.
5. I practice a lot when I'm alone.
6. You would have to masturbate into a cup.

a. *Zelig*
b. *Annie Hall*
c. *Everything You Always Wanted to Know About Sex . . .*
d. *Hannah and Her Sisters*
e. *Stardust Memories*
f. *Love and Death*

478. In five of his films, a Woody Allen character actually gets married during the course of the movie. In another four films, a Woody Allen character is seen with an ex-wife, sometimes in flashbacks. In *two* films, a Woody Allen character is married from the beginning, and doesn't divorce. Still following? There are only *three* movies directed by Allen in which he is irrevocably single, with no spouse or child in sight (at least, not his). They are

    a. *Annie Hall, Sleeper, Love and Death*
    b. *Hannah and Her Sisters, Manhattan, Annie Hall*
    c. *Stardust Memories, Broadway Danny Rose, Sleeper*
    d. *Broadway Danny Rose, Bananas, A Midsummer
       Night's Sex Comedy*

479. "Nothing worth knowing can be understood with the
mind . . . everything really valuable has to enter you through a
different opening." Which Woody Allen character says this?
    a. Sandy Bates
    b. Isaac Davis
    c. Alvy Singer
    d. Boris Grushenko

480. Virile, wisecracking, and devilishly charming, Woody Allen
characters have always made mock-heroic pretenses to immense
sexual prowess. Out of the fourteen movies he's directed (twelve
of which he stars in), there are only *three* in which he has no sex
at all during the entire course of the movie. The three movies
are
    a. *Stardust Memories, Hannah and Her Sisters, Bananas*
    b. *Play It Again, Sam, Zelig, Manhattan*
    c. *Annie Hall, The Purple Rose of Cairo, Broadway
       Danny Rose*
    d. *Zelig, Sleeper, Broadway Danny Rose*

481. In only one movie does a Woody Allen character get a chance
to score with a nymphomaniac (the ideal match, you'd figure). "I
believe in sex as often and freely as possible," she sighs, but when
he can contain himself no longer and jumps her, she pushes him
away with an indignant "What do you take me for?" This happens in
    a. *Play It Again, Sam*
    b. *Sleeper*
    c. *Everything You Always Wanted to Know About Sex . . .*
    d. *Casino Royale*

482. "How often do you have sex?" the psychiatrist asks Annie
Hall, and she responds, "Constantly—three times a week." On
the other side of the split screen, Alvy Singer's analyst asks him
the same question. What is Alvy's response?
    a. "Hardly ever—three times a week."
    b. "Constantly—three times a week."
    c. "Hardly ever—six times a week."
    d. "Constantly—once a week."

483. "Sex without love is an empty experience." "Yes, but as far
as empty experiences go, it's one of the best." This insightful
exchange occurs between
    a. Sandy Bates and a young groupie
    b. Miles Monroe and Luna
    c. Boris Grushenko and Sonia
    d. Mickey Sachs and Holly

484. Counting wives in both present time and flashbacks, one-
night stands, one-night dates, short-term and long-term relationships, how many women has Woody gone out or been affiliated
with, *on screen*, since his debut in *What's New, Pussycat?* (This
does not count aborted pickups; the criteria here is at least one
date or one sexual encounter.)
    a. forty-five
    b. thirty-two
    c. eighty-one
    d. nineteen

Q: "Where did you learn about sex?"
A: "I'm self-taught—like my clarinet playing. I'm still learning.
I just manage to have the fundamentals down pat."
                     —The New York Times, *1972*

31

TRANQUILIZING WITH THE TRIVIAL
Woody and Television

"It's not that they throw their garbage away. They make it into television shows." — *Alvy Singer in* Annie Hall

485. The *first* film directed by Woody Allen to be aired on prime-time network television was
  a. *A Midsummer Night's Sex Comedy*, CBS, 1981
  b. *Take the Money and Run*, ABC, 1973
  c. *Sleeper*, ABC, 1975
  d. *Annie Hall*, ABC, 1978

486. Like the majority of Woody Allen movies, *Manhattan* has only made it to cable television, and then with a border cropping which means the entire picture does not cover the entire TV screen. Why is this?
  a. a defect in the tape that wound up in a million-dollar lawsuit
  b. Woody insisted the original print be shown without any distortion of the image, and this is how the movie fits on TV.

    c. Woody himself cut off the sides of the frame to focus
       more on the black-and-white photography.
    d. The space was added to remind the television viewers
       that they are not watching *Manhattan* the way it was
       meant to be seen.

487. In 1962, Woody created a TV pilot, starring Louise Lasser, Alan Alda, and Paul Hampton. Woody's highbrow humor didn't translate to Middle America at the time; ABC declined to develop the program as a series. What was the name of the pilot?
    a. "The Laughmaker"
    b. "The Sex Kitten"
    c. "A Very Disturbed Family"
    d. "Death on Prime Time"

488. In 1971, Woody Allen wrote his only TV special for PBS, "The Politics of Woody Allen," which poked fun at the Nixon administration. The main character, named Harvey Wallinger, was played by Allen, and was a mock version of Henry Kissinger. Unfortunately, the program never aired, because
    a. Henry Kissinger threatened to sue the network, Woody,
       and Rollins-Joffe Productions
    b. PBS found the special "too offensive" in its treatment of
       the Nixon administration, since the show was due to air
       in 1972, an election year
    c. Woody refused to remove three scenes PBS thought too
       controversial; hence the show was canceled
    d. PBS itself canceled the show under pressure from the
       Nixon administration, which made ominous noises about
       cutting off funds for future programming

*"**T**he problem with those talk shows is that I'm expected to be funny for an hour and a half. It's a big strain. You're at peak tension because you can't let an opportunity go by without scoring."*

—*In Eric Lax,* On Being Funny: Woody Allen and Comedy, *1975*

489. TRUE OR FALSE: Though he appeared a number of times on the "Tonight" show, Woody Allen was never a substitute host for Johnny Carson.

490. Woody Allen is featured on a television show in only one of his films—a flashback sequence to an actual talk-show clip from the mid-sixties. Who is the talk-show host interviewing him?
   a. Dick Cavett
   b. Merv Griffin
   c. Jack Paar
   d. Mike Douglas

491. One of the early hallmarks of Woody's Bergman influence is a parody he wrote of the master's *Wild Strawberries*, entitled "Strange Strawberries," reprinted in Eric Lax's 1975 book, *On Being Funny: Woody Allen and Comedy*. The sketch was for a special starring
   a. Elizabeth Taylor
   b. Sid Caesar
   c. Art Carney
   d. Dick Cavett

492. Before he completely gave up on the medium, Woody Allen wrote and starred in _____ specials of his own for television.
   a. five
   b. none
   c. one
   d. two

32

HERE'S LOOKING
AT YOU, KID
The Trouble with Endings

*"**A**s you get on in a script to the final half hour, you have to be more and more funny . . . you have to accelerate and keep the pace up and end like a house afire. You can joke around with the audience through the movie, but you have to wrap it up so they are amused or satisfied."* —As told to Eric Lax

493. Woody has always had trouble with endings, mainly when trying to strike the proper note of pathos. At the end of one movie, Woody's character was supposed to end up blood-spattered and dead on a city sidewalk. He didn't, thanks to unsupportive preview audiences. Which movie was this?
   a. *Bananas*
   b. *Annie Hall*
   c. *Stardust Memories*
   d. *Take the Money and Run*

494. "You've got to have a little faith in people" is the last line of
   a. *Manhattan*
   b. *Broadway Danny Rose*
   c. *Annie Hall*
   d. *The Purple Rose of Cairo*

495. *Sleeper* ends with Miles Monroe winning Luna, and driving down the road with her, all the while professing his disbelief in everything from science to politics. In the original ending
  a. Miles loses Luna to Erno, and tries to kill himself with a large piece of broccoli
  b. Miles wins Luna, but watches in dismay as she is transformed into an alien
  c. Erno is chased by a gigantic chicken as Miles drives off with Luna
  d. Miles loses Luna to the two designers of the Orgasmatron

496. Woody Allen has gotten married at the end of only one of his movies, and it was not the original ending. It remains, however, one of the funniest endings he ever came up with overnight. It appears in
  a. *Bananas*
  b. *Love and Death*
  c. *Broadway Danny Rose*
  d. *Everything You Always Wanted to Know About Sex . . .*

497. *But . . . We Need the Eggs* is the title of a book written about Woody by Diane Jacobs, no doubt inspired by "Most of us need the eggs." This philosophical last line of a movie was said by which Woody Allen character?
  a. Isaac Davis
  b. Mickey Sachs
  c. Alvy Singer
  d. Allan Felix

498. The last line of *Hannah and Her Sisters* is
  a. "I love you."
  b. "I'm pregnant."
  c. "Sometimes, everything just works out."
  d. "You're kidding."

33

YES, BUT HOW WELL DO YOU *REALLY* KNOW THE MOVIES?
Wrap-Up

499. A child version of Woody appears in five Allen films. Can you name the correct group?

a. *Love and Death, Radio Days, Annie Hall, Take the Money and Run, Stardust Memories*

b. *Annie Hall, Take the Money and Run, A Midsummer Night's Sex Comedy, Stardust Memories, Bananas*

c. *Take the Money and Run, Zelig, Annie Hall, Bananas, Love and Death*

d. *Stardust Memories, Love and Death, Annie Hall, Hannah and Her Sisters, Take the Money and Run*

500. In which two films does Woody appear as a stand-up comedian?

a. *Manhattan, Play It Again, Sam*

b. *Everything You Always Wanted to Know About Sex . . . , Stardust Memories*

c. *Hannah and Her Sisters, Love and Death*

d. *Broadway Danny Rose, Annie Hall*

501. For all of Woody's New York filming, he only rides the subway once . . . and is terrorized. In which movie does he ride?

a. *Annie Hall*
b. *Bananas*
c. *Hannah and Her Sisters*
d. *Stardust Memories*

502. In a 1987 *Rolling Stone* interview with William Geist, Woody claims to have not driven a car in twenty-five years, with the exception of a single shot in *Annie Hall* . . . in which Alvy Singer smashes up two cars and lands in jail. As much as Woody might like to forget his prowess behind a steering wheel, there *is* one more movie in which he drives. Which one?
a. *Stardust Memories*
b. *Hannah and Her Sisters*
c. *Broadway Danny Rose*
d. *A Midsummer Night's Sex Comedy*

"Psychoanalysis helps but not as much as you want it to. I've been at it for thirteen years, three, four times a week. I've never been able to come up with any kind of single, jarring insight, although I always hoped for one." —Seventeen, *1972*

503. In how many of his movies does Woody appear in psycho-analysis?
a. four
b. three
c. six
d. two

504. Richard Nixon somehow wound up in two of Woody's mov-ies, neither of them as a performer, of course. Nixon can be glimpsed in
a. *Zelig, Annie Hall*
b. *The Purple Rose of Cairo, Manhattan*
c. *Sleeper, Take the Money and Run*
d. *Bananas, Zelig*

505. Match Woody's occupation to the movie in which he played it. (There's a trick, however: one occupation has *two* answers. . . .)

1. stockbroker   a. *Annie Hall*
2. film director   b. *Hannah and Her Sisters*
3. TV writer   c. *Manhattan*
4. TV producer   d. *Broadway Danny Rose*
5. press agent   e. *Stardust Memories*
6. film critic   f. *A Midsummer Night's Sex Comedy*
                        g. *Play It Again, Sam*

506. Well known for his love of esoteric humor, Woody has invoked specific scenes from Sergei Eisenstein's *Battleship Potemkin* in two of his own films. Which ones?
   a. *Take the Money and Run, Everything You Always Wanted to Know About Sex* . . .
   b. *Love and Death, Bananas*
   c. *Sleeper, Zelig*
   d. *The Purple Rose of Cairo, Take the Money and Run*

507. Woody actually appears on a cross in two movies—once in a recurring dream and another time as his "conception of myself as a child." The movies are
   a. *Take the Money and Run, Annie Hall*
   b. *Sleeper, Zelig*
   c. *Love and Death, Bananas*
   d. *Hannah and Her Sisters, Play It Again, Sam*

508. Fear of marriage may be a recurring theme of Woody's, but Woody had kids in a few films nonetheless. In which movie listed below did Woody *not* have kids?
   a. *Sleeper*
   b. *Take the Money and Run*
   c. *Hannah and Her Sisters*
   d. *Manhattan*

Woody and (movie) family. *Courtesy of ABC Video Enterprises*

509. To date, the top-grossing Woody Allen movie, at least in the United States, is
   a. *Hannah and Her Sisters*
   b. *Manhattan*
   c. *Love and Death*
   d. *Annie Hall*

510. Through 1987, Woody Allen has been nominated for nine Oscars, of which he has won three. (Not that he seems to care, of course; the awards ceremony falls on a Monday night . . . the same night Woody plays clarinet at Michael's Pub, an engagement he has never broken to attend the Oscars.) For which of the following two films did he only receive a nomination for original screenplay?
   a. *Interiors, Zelig*
   b. *Manhattan, The Purple Rose of Cairo*
   c. *Broadway Danny Rose, Annie Hall*
   d. *Hannah and Her Sisters, Stardust Memories*

If you have a problem with any of these answers, you can
always find Woody here. *Courtesy of Christine Demkowych*

ANSWERS

EARLY DAYS

1. b. This is also the birthday of Virgil Starkwell in *Take the Money and Run*.
2. a. Haywood Allen is also a possibility, though Woody isn't telling. In one of his comic routines, Woody tells a bully to "call me by my real name: Master Haywood Allen."
3. d
4. c
5. c
6. d. In Lee Guthrie's 1978 biography, *Woody Allen*, Woody notes that he never actually failed a college course. "It was always a very definite D. It meant you seemed to know what you were doing, but they really didn't want to pass you."
7. True. He has a married sister (yes, she has red hair), a teacher named Letty, one of the few people he will trust to screen his written work. On one of his stand-up albums, an audience member asks if Woody is an only child. "Yes," he replies. "I have a sister."
8. d
9. a

10. a. Gelbart has since gone on to create the hit TV series "M*A*S*H," not to mention scores of other TV shows and films. Woody did write with Mel Brooks and Neil Simon (as well as with Gelbart) on Sid Caesar's "Your Show of Shows."

11. c

12. b. Merrick brought it to the stage after Max Gordon, who had asked Woody to write an original play, passed on *Water*. In a memorable exchange recounted in Eric Lax's *On Being Funny: Woody Allen and Comedy*, Merrick, neatly clad in blue suit and tie, suggested to the more casually dressed Woody that he change a line. "David," Woody said, "I've made over a million dollars in my life by not listening to men in suits."

13. False. In the mid-1950s, Woody was managed by Harvey Meltzer of the William Morris Agency, whose main claim to fame was signing Woody for NBC-TV's "Colgate Comedy Hour." Since then, Charles Joffe and Jack Rollins have signed millions of dollars' worth of deals for Woody on a handshake basis. In the early sixties Joffe even spent part of his wedding night watching Woody perform.

14. c. The magic night came early in 1964. On one of his nightclub records, Woody humorously paid homage to Feldman's interest in him ("He was a short man with red hair and glasses."). The day after Feldman discovered Woody, an assistant showed up in the Rollins-Joffe offices. By the time he walked away, Woody had a thirty-five-thousand-dollar contract to write *What's New, Pussycat?*

15. c. Palomar was a short-lived subsidiary of ABC Pictures.

16. 1-d, 2-g, 3-e, 4-b, 5-a, 6-c, 7-f. Astute observers will note that Victor Shakopopolis was also the name of Woody's character in *What's New, Pussycat?*

THE NIGHTCLUB YEARS: Stand-up Woody

Complete the Quote

Q1. standing ovation

Q2. five

Q3. baseball players (specifically, Willie Mays)
Q4. the space program
Q5. hickey

17. b. In "scoring" the moose deceived the insurance salesman into believing he was a human customer. A strategic pause fooled listeners into actually believing that the moose had scored sexually before Woody deflated expectations with the punch line.
18. a
19. d. Tear gas doesn't work. The kidnappers later escape from prison posing as an immense charm bracelet!
20. c. They also "bronzed his baby shoes," according to another anecdote.
21. c
22. d. "I was the best five-year-old Stanley anyone had ever seen," Woody notes.
23. a
24. b
25. d
26. b
27. d
28. c. In *Annie Hall*, Woody does mention that the last time he drank too much, he tried to pull his pants over his head.
29. b
30. c
31. 1-b, 2-e, 3-f, 4-a, 5-d, 6-c, 7-g
32. c. In real life, he was a motion-picture major.
33. a
34. a. The overdose of Mah-Jongg tiles, according to the routine, was her supposed reaction to his divorce. But in *Annie Hall*, in Woody's college routine, she does O.D. on the tiles after he flunks out.
35. d
36. d
37. d
38. d
39. i) counterclockwise; ii) "I know, I know"; iii) rains on me

40. c
41. c
42. b
43. a
44. d
45. b

WHAT'S NEW, PUSSYCAT?

46. True. Producer Charles Feldman hired Woody to rewrite a sex comedy that had already undergone several drafts, the most recent by I. A. L. Diamond. Bought years earlier for Cary Grant, the script was completely rewritten by Woody for Warren Beatty, who was living at Feldman's Beverly Hills house at the time. When Beatty became unavailable due to another commitment, Feldman found Peter O'Toole. Having recently completed roles in sprawling epics like *Lawrence of Arabia* and *Lord Jim*, O'Toole found *Pussycat* a refreshing change of pace.
47. c
48. d
49. b. Burton and O'Toole had recently appeared together in *Becket*.
50. b
51. a
52. b
53. c
54. a
55. d
56. d. Andress, you may recall, was just coming off of *Dr. No*, and it is probable that a lot of people wished to be her personal friend.
57. b. Though Woody was a top nightclub comic, on *Pussycat*'s star-studded set he was, in his words, "a flea compared to the others." He lost dozens of scenes to the more established O'Toole and Sellers; his original writing is barely intact in the final script.
58. b. In a white snakeskin jumpsuit, no less.

59. c
60. a

WHAT'S UP, TIGER LILY?

61. b
62. False. AIP, Hollywood's mid-sixties capital of schlock, was known
    for its quickie exploitation pics and its indulgence of young tal-
    ent. AIP's Oriental counterpart, Toho Films, had produced the
    film, a bad Bond spoof, and was counting on AIP to bolster the
    film with the drive-in crowd. Watching the film in a screening
    room, however, producer Henry Saperstein found it too awful
    to take; he was instead inspired to have Woody redub the dia-
    logue after he himself began shouting back jokes to the screen.
63. c
64. d
65. a
66. c. Saperstein also inserted unrelated footage from other Japa-
    nese movies, stretching the film to seventy-nine minutes, nine-
    teen minutes longer than Woody ever anticipated. For this sort
    of tampering, Saperstein was rewarded with the lawsuit.
67. b
68. c
69. a
70. c
71. c. Louise Lasser, whose voice was also used, and Woody hilar-
    iously "interrupt" the film: the audience is sure the film has
    broken, then discovers the problem is due to Woody and Louise
    trying to have an adulterous affair in the projection room.
72. d
73. c
74. a
75. b
76. c
77. b

CASINO ROYALE

78. a
79. b
80. d. The original writers included Terry Southern, Ben Hecht, and Billy Wilder. Woody's six months in London yielded approximately one week of actual acting work. Supposedly, Woody wrote the two scenes he appeared in, as well as the climactic casino scene.
81. c
82. b
83. d
84. c
85. a
86. b
87. a
88. c. O'Toole was paid with a case of champagne for his efforts.
89. d
90. d
91. a
92. d. At one point, Charles Feldman is reported to have said, "I can't stop it now," referring to the film's runaway budget, which eventually resulted in the movie being dubbed Columbia's "little *Cleopatra*."

THE PLAY'S THE THING: Woody in the Theater

93. c
94. b
95. c
96. d
97. d
98. c
99. b—as indicated in Woody's closing quote in chapter 6
100. c

101. d
102. a
103. False. He deduces it by smelling Kleinman.
104. b
105. c
106. a
107. d
108. b
109. d. An award-winning 1959 parody of *The Seventh Seal*, made by UCLA students, does have its heroes defeating Death at badminton. This film is occasionally run on cable television before Woody Allen movies.
110. b
111. True
112. c
113. d

TAKE THE MONEY AND RUN

114. c. New York proved too expensive. The prison scenes were shot in notorious San Quentin, where Woody made sure to keep his distance from the prisoners.
115. a. This scene was moved up by editor Ralph Rosenblum from the middle of the movie. Rosenblum noted that many of the film's scenes could be juggled at will without losing plot sense.
116. c
117. d. On his *second* attempt, prisoners forget to tell him it's off, leaving Virgil haplessly by himself in the middle of the yard.
118. a
119. c. Virgil finally steps on his own glasses after unknowingly revealing his next bank heist to two police officers in the booth behind him.
120. b
121. a. "I'm not with the Philharmonic" is his deadpan confession when she arrives at the prison.

122. b. A man from the Ajax Windset Company, for those whose
     lives are affected by such things. Woody also alludes to insur-
     ance salesmen in *Love and Death* (see chapter 13), when he
     notes that there are a lot worse things than Death: "Anyone
     who's ever spent an evening with an insurance salesman will
     know what I mean."
123. b. ". . . you know, if both parties are mature and liberal."
124. d
125. d
126. c
127. a
128. b
129. 1-e, 2-g, 3-f, 4-a, 5-c, 6-b, 7-d
130. a. And he delivers a solemn explanation of the Passover holi-
     day.
131. False. It is "I only wanted a tie."
132. d. He *wants* to stab her with the knife, but plunges a turkey
     leg into her instead. And he does send dynamite . . . packed
     into candles.
133. c
134. a
135. d
136. b. Woody claims his father's mother's side of the family bore
     a resemblance to Groucho Marx.

BANANAS

137. a
138. c. Grimsby is seen on "Eyewitness News," while Dunphy is
     Howard Cosell's "Wild World of Sports" anchor.
139. b
140. a
141. d
142. c
143. b
144. d

145. d
146. Carlos Montalban
147. b
148. b
149. d
150. c
151. a
152. b. He does slam a door on his friend's hand after informing him that life is so tough. "See what I mean?" he notes.
153. a
154. a. The judge, though, says he is incorrect. "Oh yeah?" asks Fielding. "Which one?"
155. c
156. c
157. d

PLAY IT AGAIN, SAM

Complete the Quote and Name the Participants

Q1. begged them to / said by Allan to Linda

Q2. having relations / said by Allan, bemoaning his wife's reasons for their divorce

Q3. the manual / an ecstatic Allan, to himself, after making love with Linda

Q4. memories; sidewalks / a pompous Allan tries too hard to impress, on his disastrous blind date

Q5. child / said by a panting Allan to a buxom blonde on the dance floor; fortunately, she doesn't appear to hear him

158. c
159. d. Eventually, she is seen riding a motorcycle clinging to the back of a blond he-man. "We're divorced two weeks, she's dating a Nazi," Allan exclaims.
160. False. The play opened with Bogart rejecting Mary Astor at the end of *The Maltese Falcon*.
161. c

162. c. Linda, though, tells Sharon the truth about the divorce. "She's not dead?" asks Sharon. "Technically not," replies Allan. "We're not dating."

163. d. "Oh, a bourbon man," Sharon responds coolly. Allan is less than thrilled when Linda, unable to find bourbon, brings him a glass of water.

164. c
165. b
166. b
167. a
168. c
169. b
170. c
171. d
172. a
173. a
174. c

GETTING EVEN: Fiction Collection No. 1

175. d
176. d
177. a
178. 1-c, 2-d, 3-b, 4-e, 5-a, 6-f
179. c
180. b
181. c
182. a
183. c
184. a. "Is that peaceful enough for you?" the rabbi chuckles.
185. d
186. False. Both players claim checkmate.
187. c
188. b
189. a

190. d
191. b
192. d

EVERYTHING YOU ALWAYS WANTED TO KNOW ABOUT SEX (BUT WERE AFRAID TO ASK)

193. b. Gould was then thought to be a symbol of counterculture hip, a rising superstar whose luster had faded by the time Paramount realized that its original approach to the book—as a straight, cute treatment of a supposedly sensitive area—was already outdated by society's values.
194. c
195. b. The ghost scene, when the Fool speaks to his dead father, and of course, Hamlet's famous "To be or not to be" soliloquy. Here, though, it's slightly different: "TV, or not TV, that is the congestion. Consumption be done about it? Of cough, of cough."
196. a
197. d
198. a
199. d
200. a
201. b
202. d
203. c
204. b
205. True. They were Regis Philbin, Jack Barry, Robert Q. Lewis, Toni Holt, and Pamela Mason.
206. a
207. d. A mad scientist indeed.
208. c. We also see premature ejaculation in a hippopotamus and the brain of a lesbian inserted into the body of a man who works for the phone company.
209. c. Some of the other things Dr. Bernardo was noted for: res-

piration during orgasm and how to make a man impotent by hiding his hat.

210. b. Victor earlier comments on a man killed by the giant breast: "The cream slowed him up, and the milk killed him."

211. d. "We're gonna make it!" shouts Tony Randall.

212. d

213. b

214. c. The sketch is reprinted in Eric Lax's book *On Being Funny: Woody Allen and Comedy*. The end of the sketch reveals Woody, a homosexual doctor, watching the whole thing through his microscope. His secretary is the female spider, Louise Lasser. "It was one of the most hateful experiences of my life," Woody notes. "If I could've gotten any kind of ending, I would have left it in." But despite mutual efforts with Lasser, none was found.

SLEEPER

Complete the Quote and Name the Participants

Q1. brain / said by Miles, in a frightened reaction to what the government might do to his brain

Q2. spending a weekend in Beverly Hills / said by Miles upon reawakening

Q3. Sex; death / the last line of the movie, and the only institutions Miles believes in

Q4. Quakers / said by Miles to Luna, in one of their many hazardous moments

Q5. frigid / said by Luna to Miles, commenting on society in 2173

215. b

216. d. Shanker at that time was the belligerent head of the New York teachers' union.

217. a. De Gaulle is said to be a "famous chef." Those who commit crimes against the state were forced to view Cosell, here seen talking about Muhammad Ali.

218. False. He is unfrozen because the scientists need an unregistered citizen to overthrow the tyrannical government.
219. d
220. d
221. b. In an astonishing pre-Watergate forecast, however, Miles notes that Nixon was guilty of a crime so horrible all records of him were wiped out.
222. c
223. c
224. a
225. d
226. d
227. b. Luna immediately lapses into a credible Stanley Kowalski.
228. a
229. c
230. c
231. d
232. True. Woody was so enamored of the Knicks star that he wrote a cover story about Monroe for *Sport* magazine.

LOVE AND DEATH

Complete the Quote and Name the Participants

Q1. underachiever; Boris's description of God
Q2. erogenous zones; Boris flirts with Countess Alexandrovna as a jealous Count looks on. "But what about the dybbuk?" Boris asks, nodding to the Count.
Q3. The late 1700s; Boris, assuring the Countess he's ready for sex
Q4. homosexual; Boris's soliloquy on Socrates
Q5. lawyers; same as above

233. c
234. b
235. a

236. c
237. b
238. d
239. d
240. c. "What'll they do, rape Yvonne?" Boris counters, referring to his cousin. "They'll throw up."
241. a
242. d. "Once would've been nice," Voskovec mumbles, before dying.
243. a
244. a
245. d
246. b
247. a
248. c
249. b, played by Jessica Harper
250. d
251. c

WITHOUT FEATHERS: Fiction Collection No. 2

252. a
253. c
254. d
255. 1-b, 2-e, 3-d, 4-f, 5-c, 6-a
256. c
257. b
258. c
259. a
260. b
261. b
262. c
263. b
264. 1-c, 2-d, 3-a, 4-b, 5-e
265. a
266. c
267. True

THE FRONT

268. b. The blacklist was particularly interesting to Woody, since he was only in public school at the time it went into effect and was unaware of its implications. "The script expresses me politically even though I didn't write it," he told an interviewer.
269. c
270. False. There were two others as well: actors Lloyd Gough and Joshua Shelley, both of whom were blacklisted in 1952.
271. d
272. a. And then only so he could be close to a pretty girl who happened to be political. Hecky's suicide later on in the film, incidentally, is based on that of a real actor, Philip Loeb, who from 1949 to 1951 played Gertrude Berg's husband in a TV show called "The Goldbergs." Like Hecky, Loeb was blacklisted and constantly harassed; he finally took an overdose of sleeping pills.
273. c
274. c
275. d
276. a
277. c
278. True. To my knowledge Woody lags way behind De Niro, Pacino, and Nicholson in the obscenity department; if you can find one such evil word in any of Woody's films, you may let me know. Politely.

ANNIE HALL

Complete the Quote and Name the Participants

Q1. Kafkaesque; said by a *Rolling Stone* reporter to Alvy after making love. "Thank you," he replies somewhat stiffly. "It's a compliment," she adds.

Q2. raped by Cossacks; Alvy, describing to Annie the difference between Grammy Hall and *his* grandmother

Q3. Norman Rockwell painting?; Alvy's incredulous reaction to Annie's WASP family

Q4. a real Jew; said by Annie to Alvy on their first meeting

Q5. Teach gym; Alvy, reflecting on his teachers

279. b. *Anhedonia*, which means "the inability to experience pleasure," gave very little pleasure to United Artists execs. Woody held fast with the title until various screenings convinced him otherwise. *Annie & Alvy* was one of the other possible titles.

280. False. *Annie Hall* picked up Oscars for Best Picture, Best Director, Best Screenplay, and Best Actress (Diane Keaton). Woody lost out to Richard Dreyfuss, who won for *The Goodbye Girl*. Woody did win Best Director and Best Screenplay from the New York Film Critics Circle.

281. b. There are disparate reports about this. In one version, Woody took the characters from his novel and adapted them to the film. In another, Woody and Marshall Brickman were set to write a Victorian-era murder-mystery film; Woody changed his mind at the last minute and opted for a more surreal, autobiographical story.

282. b. "What is that your business!" his mother demands.

283. c. On a movie line, Alvy did request a large sock of horse manure to silence a man pontificating about Fellini.

284. a

285. d. Alvy notes this to Allison while trying to figure out the cover-up of JFK's assassination.

286. b

287. d. As proof that his difficulties with the wrong women started at an early age, Alvy notes that he fell for the Wicked Queen.

288. a

289. 1-f, 2-d, 3-g, 4-b, 5-c, 6-a, 7-e

290. a

291. d

292. b. He tells this to Alvy in his bedroom. Whereupon Alvy carefully gets up and tells him he's "due back on the planet Earth."

293. c

294. d
295. b
296. a
297. c
298. b
299. True. Another tidbit: Woody originally wanted to use his own Flatbush birthplace for the opening, but changed his mind as soon as he discovered the house under the roller coaster.
300. d. Woody told *The New York Times* in 1977: "I remember having Thanksgiving dinner at one of [Diane Keaton's] Grammies's houses. A beautiful American family. I felt I was an alien or exotic object to them, a nervous, anxiety-ridden, suspicious, wise-cracking kind of strange bird. After dinner, all these grammies sat around playing poker . . . my family would've been exchanging gunfire."

INTERIORS

301. d
302. b
303. d
304. b. She is getting ready to kill herself, though she doesn't succeed the first time.
305. a
306. b
307. c. The shooting of *Interiors* necessitated the dislodging of a number of people from their houses and apartments, since, as one man whose loft was used for the movie noted, "Woody Allen doesn't like people around when he's shooting." The other family whose summer house was used for the beach scenes was less than thrilled with the way it was treated. Mel Bourne had looked at fifty beach houses before settling on the home of the Caristos, who were away for the summer. But their daughter complained to *The New York Times* that the crew stretched a broadloom out of shape and didn't put all the wall lighting

fixtures back in place. "What's really bothering us," she noted, "is that we're missing a hand-carved Pinocchio that my father found in Italy."

308. True. Susan Morse, his assistant, took over from *Manhattan* onward.

309. c. Not that it gets him anywhere.

310. a. Geraldine Page was nominated for Best Actress and Maureen Stapleton for Best Supporting Actress. Though the film failed to win an Oscar, England's *Films and Filming* voted it Best Picture for 1978, and Geraldine Page Best Actress. The British Academy of Film and Television Art named Page Best Supporting Actress.

MANHATTAN

Complete the Quote and Name the Participants

Q1. August Strindberg; Isaac being honest with Yale

Q2. interstellar perversion; Isaac being honest with Mary

Q3. pigeons and Catholics; Isaac discussing his world view with Mary

Q4. Zelda Fitzgerald Emotional Maturity; an astonished Isaac can't believe Yale is going to leave his wife for Mary

Q5. the male organ; Mary, being honest with Isaac

311. a

312. b

313. Queensborough (or Fifty-ninth Street) Bridge

314. b. The one on Bleecker Street, and Woody's favorite pizzeria. Owner Pete Castellotti has since appeared in *Broadway Danny Rose*, *The Purple Rose of Cairo*, and *Radio Days*

315. c

316. b

317. d

318. c

319. a

320. b. Mary calls her analyst Dr. Chomsky.

Top: John's Pizzeria. *Bottom*: Inside John's, Woody has been enshrined in a virtual museum. Posing next to Woody is Pete Castellotti, owner of John's. On the wall is the ax from *Broadway Danny Rose* that Castellotti used in the movie to chase Danny Rose with. Inscribed on the blade is a note from Woody: "To my favorite hit man." *Courtesy of Todd Lane*

321. a
322. d
323. False. They met at a Knicks game, where Woody, a rabid fan, can frequently be found. The Knicks actually appear on TV briefly in *Annie Hall*.
324. d. The others: Norman Mailer, Scott Fitzgerald, Lenny Bruce, Walt Whitman, Vincent van Gogh, and Ingmar Bergman, the last whom gets Mary in severe trouble with Isaac. ("If she had made one more remark about Bergman," he tells Tracy later, "I would've knocked her other contact lens out.")
325. b
326. c. Mary manages to name Mimas, Titan, Dione, and Hyperion. If you know the others, my hat is off to you.
327. a
328. False. But Yale tells this to his wife, who springs it on a surprised Isaac near the end of the movie. Isaac just nods affirmatively.
329. d
330. They are all part of Isaac's "reasons worth living for." The others? "Potatohead Blues" by Louis Armstrong, *Sentimental Education* by Flaubert, and . . . Tracy's face.

STARDUST MEMORIES

Complete the Quote and Name the Participants

Q1. the loyal opposition; Sandy, making a point to his studio executives
Q2. Schopenhauer; Dorrie, to Sandy's pickup attempt
Q3. on their wedding night; Sandy's one classical-music joke, as told to Daisy
Q4. Marxist; one of Sandy's many strange fans
Q5. American; Sandy expressing his political views

331. a
332. a
333. c

334. b
335. c
336. b
337. c
338. a. Woody himself has said this repeatedly.
339. c
340. a. According to the movie, Sandy has seen it five times.
341. c
342. False. He makes this comment after he is recognized by a woman who once played his mother in a movie. "I had my face done, my breasts done, I had my ass done, I got some procaine and silicone, some nipping and tucking," she tells him.
343. d
344. d. Crist plays a cabaret patron, while Kissel plays Sandy's manager. Crist once held a weekend seminar, in honor of Woody's films, similar to the one depicted in *Stardust Memories*.

SIDE EFFECTS: Fiction Collection No. 3

345. a
346. c
347. False. He will begin to sound like Jerry Lewis
348. b
349. c
350. d
351. c, where he is running over a rocky, barren plain from *tener* ("to have"), a large, hairy, irregular verb
352. b
353. a
354. b
355. c
356. b
357. d
358. c

359. a

360. a. The daughter falls out of love with him when she develops a brother complex about Harold. After Harold marries her mother, she comes on to him again, since he now represents a father figure.

A MIDSUMMER NIGHT'S SEX COMEDY

Complete the Quote and Name the Participants

Q1. causes it; said by Andrew to his good friend Dr. Maxwell.

Q2. the death of hope; Dr. Maxwell's world philosophy, as told to Andrew

Q3. missed opportunities; as told by Andrew to Ariel

361. True

362. b. Part of the problem with Woody's desire to act in more serious roles is that fans have mistaken serious, emotional moments like this one as another of Woody's slapstick jokes.

363. a

364. d. Three hundred too many, as it turns out.

365. c

366. b

367. c

368. d. Using some of the lessons taught to her by Dulcy.

369. a

370. c

371. d

372. True. He makes a final ghostly appearance at the end.

373. a

374. c. No one has sex with the person they arrived with. It's obvious by the end of the film that Andrew and Adrian will resume *their* sexual relationship, having at last worked out their sexual problems . . . and confessed their guilt.

ZELIG

375. b
376. d
377. a
378. b. This was Woody's send-up of Warren Beatty's *Reds*, in which narration is supplied by leading personalities of the period.
379. c
380. b
381. d. In a 1978 *Newsweek* article, Marshall Brickman noted that Woody saves string. You may also recall that Ivan, Boris Grushenko's Neanderthal brother in *Love and Death*, did too.
382. b
383. a
384. a
385. True
386. c
387. d
388. c
389. a. "Lou Zelig" is the on-deck batter.
390. a
391. c

BROADWAY DANNY ROSE

392. c
393. d. The "Jascha Heifetz of her instrument," as Danny Rose describes her in the movie, is actually Gloria Parker, a musical prodigy who made her debut at the age of five playing violin onstage at the Brooklyn Academy of Music. Her grandfather, who learned glasspiel—or "singing glasses"—in Czechoslovakia, passed the art on to her, and she became instantly enamored of it. "Nobody can poke fun at the glasses," she told *The New York Times* in a March 1984 article. "Benjamin Frank-

lin introduced them to America in 1751. They are part of our heritage. And now, through the movie, the whole world can see them in the twentieth century, and I will be the person affixed to them."

394. d
395. b
396. a
397. b. Celia looked like a "reptile in the zoo."
398. b. Rollins also appeared in *Stardust Memories*.
399. True
400. d. Joe refers to him as "Lou Canola."
401. a
402. d
403. b
404. a. "Oh, a professional man," Danny notes.
405. c
406. c

THE PURPLE ROSE OF CAIRO

Complete the Quote and Name the Participants

Q1. midget; said by the fictional character Tom Baxter
Q2. fictional character; said by Cecilia to her sister
Q3. the movies; said by Cecilia to her husband

407. b
408. a
409. d
410. c
411. a. Woody found Keaton's modern-day sensibility too contemporary for the requirements of the character. Keaton was gone after two weeks. Juliet Taylor's discovery of Daniels saved Woody from writing himself into the movie, which he didn't want to do. "I'm not the matinee-idol type," he said. "If he

asked me to work with him again, I would in a minute," Daniels told *Moviegoer*, 1985. "My whole thing as an actor is to have a director I can trust, and if you can't trust Woody Allen, you can't trust anybody."

412. a

413. a

414. d

415. c

416. b

417. d. At one point, one of the other characters does try to step off the screen, but can't. Why only Baxter can remains part of the magic of the movies. . . .

418. a. She is also surprised to find that her "night on the town" in Manhattan whirls by in three minutes, thanks to a dissolve/montage effect.

419. c. This is the reason he professes. As a movie character, though, it's probable he's never made love, since motion-picture censorship codes would have prohibited any such scenes at the time.

420. b

421. a

HANNAH AND HER SISTERS

Complete the Quote and Name the Participants

Q1. exchange gunshots; Mickey, remembering his nightmarish first date with Holly

Q2. the Nuremberg trials; Mickey's parting line to Holly after that first date

Q3. resilient; Mickey, to Holly, now his wife

Q4. Actors Equity; Hannah's father, in a moment of jealousy, bitterly joking about whether he's Hannah's real father

422. c

423. a
424. True. The closest she comes is when Holly's screenplay reveals a knowledge of Elliot and Hannah's marriage that could only have resulted from talks with Lee. But Holly maintains her script is fictitious, and not based on them.
425. c
426. b
427. d
428. a
429. b
430. d
431. c
432. a
433. b. *Duck Soup*, to be exact. "Any world that could've created the Marx Brothers can't be all that bad," Mickey surmises.

RADIO DAYS

434. b
435. d
436. b. This after Sidney left her abandoned in a car at Breezy Point late at night . . . scared out of his wits by Orson Welles's "War of the Worlds."
437. a. "What's Pearl Harbor?" Sally asks later.
438. b. He also winds up eating pork chops and french fries, which leaves him terribly ill.
439. d
440. b
441. b
442. a. Joe abandons his pursuit of the sacred ring after this harrowing incident, triggered when he refers to the rabbi as "my faithful Indian companion."
443. 1-c, 2-e, 3-d, 4-a, 5-b

GIRLS, GIRLS, GIRLS: The Women
in Woody's Films

444. b. Neither appeared in *Bananas* either.
445. a
446. b
447. d
448. c. In real life Hemingway seemed every inch the ingenue she played with such tenderness in *Manhattan*. According to Woody, she spent her days on the set "doing her homework, jumping rope, and drinking her health-food concoctions." She also, Woody reports, "had an inordinate amount of trouble with any kind of intimate moment." As for her character losing Woody to the neurotic and brainy Diane Keaton character, Hemingway told *The New York Times*: "I couldn't see why he would like a person who was so—obnoxious."
449. 1-c, 2-e, 3-g, 4-a, 5-f, 6-b, 7-d. Rampling played the troubled Dorrie, Streep was Isaac's ex-wife-turned-lesbian, Haggerty the free-thinking Dulcy, Hurt the troubled young writer, Redgrave the Queen—Fisher Holly's best friend (and rival), and Weaver a walk-on as Alvy Singer's date.
450. a
451. c. Hershey told this to *The New York Times* following the release of *Hannah and Her Sisters*.
452. d. Page was in *Interiors*.
453. c. Woody told this to *The New York Times* in 1969, when Allen and Lasser were still married.

I DON'T WANT TO ACHIEVE IMMORTALITY
THROUGH MY WORK: I Want to Achieve it
Through Not Dying

454. d
455. c
456. b. The Fool is guillotined in the first sketch of *Sex*, Boris Gru-

shenko is executed and taken away in a Dance of Death at the
conclusion of *Love and Death*, and Jimmy Bond blows up himself (and the rest of the world) at the end of *Casino Royale*.

457. c. Mickey's rifle misfires in *Hannah*, while Boris, hanging from
the rafters with a rope around his neck, is suddenly seized by
an urge to live in *Love and Death*.

458. a. This after Boris is challenged to a duel to the death by the
Count. In *Casino Royale*, Jimmy Bond notes that doctors do
not permit "bullets to enter my body."

459. 1-d, 2-e, 3-c, 4-a, 5-b

460. c. He is blown Down Under by Peter Sellers.

461. False. While Jimmy Bond escapes execution in *Casino Royale*,
Boris Grushenko is not so lucky at the end of *Love and Death*—
though an angel appeared the night before assuring him God
was taking care of everything.

462. b

463. d. For a similar poke at insurance salesmen, see question 252.

ONE BIG HAPPY FAMILY

464. b. Aiello appeared as Bea Arthur's cheating husband in *The
Floating Light Bulb*, as Cecilia's loser husband in *The Purple
Rose of Cairo*, and as a Mafia hit man in *Radio Days*. He also
appeared briefly in *The Front*. His cameo in *Annie Hall* wound
up on the cutting-room floor. Lou Jacobi starred as Walter
Hollander in the Broadway version of *Don't Drink the Water*,
and was caught donning women's clothing in *Everything You
Always Wanted to Know About Sex* . . . , in the sketch entitled
"Are Transvestites Homosexual?"

465. False. Brickman, then head writer for Johnny Carson, did
collaborate on the script with Woody in 1971–72. Brickman
told Eric Lax that "no one else thought it was funny," and it
was never made.

466. a

467. c
468. d
469. a
470. c. John Doumanian is executive producer of "Saturday Night Live."
471. c. Stallone briefly terrorizes Fielding Mellish on the subway.
472. True. Cosell also appears at Danny Rose's table, next to Milton Berle, watching Lou Canova sing. On their first meeting, in 1966, Woody kept Cosell from joining a high-stakes poker game already in progress, because it was "too crowded." "When you eat dinner with Howard Cosell," Woody once said, "he broadcasts the meal."
473. c
474. b

IT'S NOT THE QUANTITY THAT COUNTS, BUT THE QUALITY

475. d. From *Play It Again, Sam*
476. a. Alvy takes this surreal tour with Annie and his friend Max. The scene was one of many funny bits cut from the movie.
477. 1-b, 2-e, 3-c, 4-a, 5-f, 6-d
478. c
479. b. In other words, Isaac implies that Mary thinks too much.
480. d. While it's conceivable that Leonard Zelig sleeps with Eudora Fletcher, no allusions whatsoever are made to this. Miles and Luna don't stop *fighting* until the end of *Sleeper*. And Danny Rose is too busy staying out of trouble and falling in love with Tina.
481. a. The part of the nympho is played by superstar model Viva, in a bravura performance.
482. a
483. c. From *Love and Death*. In *Stardust Memories*, a groupie who surprises Sandy Bates in bed overrules his protests against

their one-night stand, telling him, "Sex with no love is better than no sex at all, right?"

484. b. A careful screening of all the films and observation of the strict criteria bear me out. Trust me.

TRANQUILIZING WITH THE TRIVIAL:
Woody and Television

485. c. Woody does not like to sell his movies to network television because he fears overexposure, commercials, and TV edits. *Take the Money and Run* didn't run until 1978. *A Midsummer Night's Sex Comedy* ran only as a CBS late movie, and not till 1986.

486. b

487. a

488. c. PBS did have questions about the show, but would have run it had Woody allowed the removal of the following scenes: an obscene gesture by Hubert Humphrey (taken out of context from somewhere); a scene where a divorced Wallinger is seen escorting a nun, Sister Mary Elizabeth Smith ("He's an unbelievable swinger; a freak," Smith says of Wallinger); and a scene where Wallinger admits to turning down seductive invitations from Pat Nixon when her husband was out of the country. Woody claimed no great political insight for the show, and readily agreed it was in bad taste. "But it's hard to do anything about the administration that *wouldn't* be in bad taste," he noted. The underlying feeling was that the Nixon administration itself was responsible for PBS's hesitation. At any rate, Woody, who worked for scale on the project, turned his back on television forever.

489. False. Though he has not appeared on talk shows for some fifteen years, in the sixties, when Woody was trying to build a national following, he was a frequent guest on the "Tonight" show. In the summer of 1964, Woody hosted the show for a week while Carson was on vacation.

490. a. Cavett appears in *Annie Hall*.
491. c
492. d. One in 1968 with Billy Graham, the Fifth Dimension, and Candice Bergen; the other in 1970 with Liza Minnelli. Neither was a big hit.

HERE'S LOOKING AT YOU, KID:
The Trouble with Endings

493. d. Woody wanted a *Bonnie and Clyde*–style ending to the Virgil Starkwell saga, but was quickly overridden by editor Ralph Rosenblum and preview audiences.
494. a. It is said by Tracy, before leaving for London.
495. c
496. a. Originally, Woody, the inadvertent rebel hero, is invited to give a revolutionary speech at Columbia University, but is interrupted by a black mob intent on killing him. A bomb goes off, he ducks for cover, and when he gets up, covered in black from soot, he is mistaken for a brother by three black men with rifles.
497. c
498. b

YES, BUT HOW WELL DO YOU *REALLY*
KNOW THE MOVIES?: Wrap-up

499. a
500. d
501. b
502. c
503. a. He appears on the couch in *Take the Money and Run*, *Bananas*, *Annie Hall*, and *Zelig*.
504. c
505. 1-f, 2-e, 3-a and c, 4-b, 5-d, 6-e

506. b. The baby carriage flying down the steps in *Bananas*, and sheep being led to the slaughter, as well as a montage of stone lion statues, in *Love and Death*.

507. c. In *Love and Death*, Woody reports that he had a "different conception of myself as a child." In *Bananas*, nuns battle each other for a parking space for their crucifixion; Woody is on one of the crosses.

508. a

509. d

510. b. Woody was also nominated for Best Director for *Interiors* and Best Screenplay for *Broadway Danny Rose*. He won both directing and writing awards for *Annie Hall* (which won Best Picture for 1977), and best original screenplay for *Hannah and Her Sisters*.

WOODY'S WORKS

FILMS

What's New, Pussycat? (1965). Director: Clive Donner. Screenplay: Woody Allen. Producer: Charles Feldman. Director of Photography: Jean Badal. Editor: Fergus McDonnell. Music: Burt Bacharach. United Artists/Famous Artists, 108 minutes. Featured Cast: Woody Allen, Peter O'Toole, Romy Schneider, Paula Prentiss, Peter Sellers, Capucine, Ursula Andress.

What's Up, Tiger Lily? (1966). Original title: *Key of Keys*, produced by Toho (1964), directed by Senkichi Taniguchi. American version: Executive Producer: Henry Saperstein. Associate Producer: Woody Allen. English Script and Dubbing: Woody Allen, Louise Lasser, Mickey Rose, Len Maxwell, Julie Bennett, Bryna Wilson. Editor: Richard Krown. Music: Lovin' Spoonful. American International Pictures, 80 minutes.

Casino Royale (1967). Directors: John Huston, Ken Hughes, Val Guest, Robert Parrish, Joe McGrath. Screenplay: Wolf Mankowitz, John Law, Michael Sayers, from the novel by Ian Fleming. Produc-

233

ers: Charles K. Feldman, Jerry Bresler. Directors of Photography: Jack Hilyard, John Wilcox, Nicholas Roeg. Production Designer: Michael Stringer. Music: Burt Bacharach. Columbia/Famous Artists, 131 minutes. Featured Cast: Woody Allen, David Niven, Peter Sellers, Ursula Andress, Orson Welles, Joanna Pettit, Daliah Lavi, Deborah Kerr, William Holden, Charles Boyer, Jean-Paul Belmondo, John Huston, George Raft, Jacqueline Bisset.

Don't Drink the Water (1969). Director: Howard Morris. Screenplay: R. S. Allen and Harvey Bullock, from Woody Allen's play. Producer: Charles H. Joffe. Associate Producer: Jack Grossberg. Executive Producer: Joseph E. Levine. Director of Photography: Harvey Genkins. Editorial Supervision: Ralph Rosenblum. Music: Pat Williams. An Avco Embassy Film, 98 minutes. Featured Cast: Jackie Gleason, Estelle Parsons, Ted Bessell, Joan Delaney, Michael Constantine.

Take the Money and Run (1969). Directed by Woody Allen. Written by Woody Allen and Mickey Rose. Producer: Charles H. Joffe for Palomar Pictures. Director of Photography: Lester Shorr. Editor: James T. Heckert, Ralph Rosenblum. Art Director: Fred Harpman. Special Effects: A. D. Flowers. Music: Marvin Hamlisch. Released by ABC Pictures, 85 minutes. Featured Cast: Woody Allen, Janet Margolin, Jackson Beck, Marcel Hillaire, Jacqueline Hyde.

Bananas (1970). Directed by Woody Allen. Written by Woody Allen and Mickey Rose. Producer: Jack Grossberg. Executive Producer: Charles H. Joffe. Production Designer: Ed Wittstein. Associate Producer: Ralph Rosenblum. Editor: Ron Kalish. Director of Photography: Andrew M. Costikyan. Special Effects: Don B. Courtney. Music: Marvin Hamlisch. Released through United Artists, 81 minutes. Featured Cast: Woody Allen, Louise Lasser, Carlos Montalban, Howard Cosell.

Play It Again, Sam (1972). Directed by Herbert Ross. Written by Woody Allen, from his play. Producer: Arthur P. Jacobs. Executive Producer: Charles H. Joffe. Director of Photography: Owen Roiz-

man. Editor: Marion Rothman. Music: Billy Goldenberg. Production
Designer: Ed Wittstein. A Paramount Pictures release, 85 minutes.
Featured Cast: Woody Allen, Diane Keaton, Tony Roberts, Jerry
Lacy.

*Everything You Always Wanted to Know About Sex (But Were
Afraid to Ask)* (1972). Directed by Woody Allen. Written by Woody
Allen from the book by David M. Reuben. Produced by Charles H.
Joffe. Executive Producer: Jack Brodsky. Associate Producer: Jack
Grossberg. Production Design: Dale Hennesy. Director of Photog-
raphy: David Walsh. Editor: Eric Albertson. A United Artists re-
lease, 87 minutes. Featured Cast: Woody Allen, Louise Lasser, Lynn
Redgrave, Gene Wilder, Burt Reynolds, Tony Randall, John Car-
radine, Lou Jacobi.

Sleeper (1973). Directed by Woody Allen. Written by Woody Allen
and Marshall Brickman. Producer: Jack Grossberg. Executive Producer: Charles H. Joffe. Director of Photography: David M. Walsh.
Editor: Ralph Rosenblum. Set Designer: Dianne Wager. Special Effects: A. D. Flowers. Music by Woody Allen, with the Preservation
Hall Band and the New Orleans Funeral Ragtime Orchestra. A Rollins-Joffe production, released through United Artists, 88 minutes.
Featured Cast: Woody Allen, Diane Keaton, John Beck, Mary
Gregory.

Love and Death (1975). Written and directed by Woody Allen. Producer: Charles H. Joffe. Associate Producer: Fred T. Gallo. Executive Producer: Martin Poll. Editors: Ralph Rosenblum, Ron Kalish.
Special Effects: Kit West, Peter Dawson. Music: S. Prokofiev. Director of Photography: Ghislain Cloquet. A United Artists film, 85
minutes. Featured Cast: Woody Allen, Diane Keaton, Jessica Harper, James Tolkan.

The Front (1976). Directed by Martin Ritt. Written by Walter Bernstein. Producer: Martin Ritt. Executive Producer: Charles H. Joffe.
Associate Producer: Robert Greenhut. Director of Photography: Michael Chapman. Music: Dave Grusin. Editor: Sidney Levin. Released

through Columbia Pictures, 94 minutes. Featured Cast: Woody Allen, Andrea Marcovicci, Zero Mostel, Herschel Bernardi.

Annie Hall (1977). Directed by Woody Allen. Written by Woody Allen and Marshall Brickman. Producer: Charles H. Joffe. Executive Producer: Robert Greenhut. Director of Photography: Gordon Willis. Editor: Ralph Rosenblum. Art Director: Mel Bourne. A United Artists release, 93 minutes. Featured Cast: Woody Allen, Diane Keaton, Tony Roberts, Paul Simon, Carol Kane, Janet Margolin, Colleen Dewhurst, Christopher Walken, Shelley Duvall.

Interiors (1978). Written and directed by Woody Allen. Producer: Charles H. Joffe. Executive Producer: Robert Greenhut. Director of Photography: Gordon Willis. Editor: Ralph Rosenblum. Production Designer: Mel Bourne. A United Artists release, 93 minutes. Featured Cast: Kristen Griffith, Diane Keaton, Marybeth Hurt, E. G. Marshall, Geraldine Page, Sam Waterston, Richard Jordan, Maureen Stapleton.

Manhattan (1979). Directed by Woody Allen. Written by Woody Allen and Marshall Brickman. Producer: Charles H. Joffe. Executive Producer: Robert Greenhut. Director of Photography: Gordon Willis. Editor: Susan E. Morse. Production Designer: Mel Bourne. Music: George Gershwin, adapted and arranged by the New York Philharmonic. A United Artists release, 96 minutes. Featured Cast: Woody Allen, Mariel Hemingway, Meryl Streep, Michael Murphy.

Stardust Memories (1980). Written and directed by Woody Allen. Producer: Robert Greenhut. Executive Producers: Jack Rollins and Charles H. Joffe. Director of Photography: Gordon Willis. Production Designer: Mel Bourne. Editor: Susan E. Morse. Piano music arranged and performed by Dick Hyman. A United Artists release, 89 minutes. Featured Cast: Woody Allen, Jessica Harper, Charlotte Rampling, Marie-Christine Barrault, Tony Roberts.

A Midsummer Night's Sex Comedy (1982). Written and directed by Woody Allen. Producer: Robert Greenhut. Executive Producer:

Charles H. Joffe. Associate Producer: Michael Peyser. Director of Photography: Gordon Willis. Editor: Susan E. Morse. Production Designer: Mel Bourne. Music: Felix Mendelssohn. An Orion Pictures release, 94 minutes. Featured Cast: Woody Allen, Mia Farrow, Julie Haggerty, Mary Steenburgen, Tony Roberts, Jose Ferrer.

Zelig (1983). Written and directed by Woody Allen. Producer: Robert Greenhut. Executive Producer: Charles H. Joffe. Associate Producer: Michael Peyser. Director of Photography: Gordon Willis. Editor: Susan E. Morse. Production Designer: Mel Bourne. Optical Effects: Joel Hyneck and Stuart Robertson. Stills Animation: Steven Plastrik and Computer Opticals, Inc. An Orion Pictures release, 79 minutes. Featured Cast: Woody Allen, Mia Farrow, Susan Sontag, Irving Howe, Dr. Bruno Bettelheim, Saul Bellow.

Broadway Danny Rose (1984). Written and directed by Woody Allen. Producer: Robert Greenhut. Executive Producer: Charles H. Joffe. Associate Producer: Michael Peyser. Director of Photography: Gordon Willis. Editor: Susan E. Morse. Production Designer: Mel Bourne. An Orion Pictures release, 85 minutes. Featured Cast: Woody Allen, Mia Farrow, Nick Apollo Forte, Corbett Monica, Howard Storm, Jack Rollins, Will Jordan, Jackie Gayle, Morty Gunty, Sandy Baron.

The Purple Rose of Cairo (1985). Written and directed by Woody Allen. Producer: Robert Greenhut. Executive Producer: Charles H. Joffe. Associate Producers: Michael Peyser and Gail Sicilia. Director of Photography: Gordon Willis. Editor: Susan E. Morse. Production Designer: Stuart Wertzel. An Orion Pictures release, 81 minutes. Featured Cast: Mia Farrow, Jeff Daniels, Dianne Wiest, Danny Aiello, Ed Herrmann, Deborah Rush, Van Johnson, Zoe Caldwell, Milo O'Shea, John Wood.

Hannah and Her Sisters (1986). Written and directed by Woody Allen. Producer: Robert Greenhut. Executive Producer: Charles H. Joffe. Director of Photography: Carlo Di Palma. Editor: Susan E. Morse. Production Designer: Santo Loquasto. An Orion Pictures release, 107 minutes. Featured Cast: Woody Allen, Mia Farrow,

Dianne Wiest, Barbara Hershey, Carrie Fisher, Sam Waterston, Max von Sydow, Tony Roberts.

Radio Days (1987). Written and directed by Woody Allen. Producer: Robert Greenhut. Executive Producer: Charles H. Joffe. Director of Photography: Carlo Di Palma. Editor: Susan E. Morse. Production Designer: Santo Loquasto. An Orion Pictures release, 92 minutes. Featured Cast: Julie Kavner, Michael Tucker, Wallace Shawn, Diane Keaton, Mia Farrow, Tony Roberts, Jeff Daniels, Danny Aiello.

THEATER

Don't Drink the Water (1966). Written by Woody Allen. Produced by David Merrick, with Charles Joffe and Jack Rollins. Directed by Stanley Prager. Featured Cast: Lou Jacobi, Kay Medford, Anita Gillette, Tony Roberts.

Play It Again, Sam (1969). Written by Woody Allen. Produced by David Merrick. Directed by Joe Hardy. Starring Woody Allen, Diane Keaton, Tony Roberts, Jerry Lacy. Presented at the Broadhurst Theater on February 11.

The Floating Light Bulb (1981). Written by Woody Allen. Produced by Richard Crinkley. Directed by Ulu Grosbard. Starring Brian Backer, Beatrice Arthur, Jack Weston, Danny Aiello, Eric Gurry, Ellen March. Presented on April 27 by the Lincoln Center Theater Company at the Vivian Beaumont Theater.

BOOKS BY WOODY ALLEN

Getting Even, Random House, 1971
Without Feathers, Random House, 1975
Side Effects, Random House, 1980

DISCOGRAPHY

Woody Allen: Colpix CP 488, 1964
Woody Allen, Vol. 2: Colpix CP 518, 1965
The Third Woody Allen Album: Capitol ST2986, n.d.
Woody Allen: The Nightclub Years, 1964–68: United Artists UA 9968, 1976
Woody Allen: Standup Comic, 1964–68: United Artists UA-LA 849–J2, 1978

THE ONE-ACT PLAYS (UNPRODUCED)

Death Knocks, 1971
Death, 1975
God, 1975